Campbell's

Quick *and* Easy
RECIPES

CRESCENT BOOKS
New York

This edition published by
Crescent Books, distributed by
Random House Value Publishing, Inc.
201 East 50th Street, New York, N.Y. 10022
Random House
New York • Toronto • London • Sydney • Auckland

Editor: Angela Rahaniotis
Graphic Design and Layout: Zapp
Photography: Studio Tormont
Photographer: Marc Bruneau
Food Preparation/Stylist: Josée Robitaille
Assistant Food Preparation/Hand Model: Marc Maula
Prop Stylist: Danielle Schneider

For sending us kitchen equipment used in recipe technique photos, a special thanks to: *Corning Incorporated,* Corning, NY; *Ekco Housewares, Inc.,* Franklin Park, IL; and *Regal Ware, Inc.*, Kewaskum, WI.

Props Courtesy of: Henry Birks and Sons, Cache Cache, Les Carreaux Ramca Ltée, La Charmille, Galerie Parchemine, La Maison d'Émilie, Marie Vermette Inc., Ogilvy, Pier 1 Imports, Pierre-Olivier Décor, Arthur Quentin, Les Tissus Télio.

This edition was produced by Campbell Soup Company's Publications Center, Campbell Soup Company, Campbell Place, Camden, New Jersey 08103-1799, U.S.A.

Campbell's QUICK AND EASY RECIPES Cookbook
Corporate Editor: Patricia Teberg
Assistant Editors: Alice Joy Carter, Margaret Romano
Editorial Assistant: Gloria J. Pinchac
Campbell Kitchens: Linda Armor

Every recipe in Campbell's QUICK AND EASY RECIPES cookbook was developed and tested in the Campbell Kitchens by professional home economists.

Pictured on the front cover, clockwise from center: Savory Chicken and Mushrooms (*recipe on page 54*), Herbed Turkey and Mushrooms (*recipe on page 78*) and Pork Mozzarella (*recipe on page 106*).

Preparation and Cooking Times: Each of these recipes was developed and tested in the Campbell Kitchens by professional home economists. Use "Prep Time" and "Cook Time" given with each recipe as guides. The preparation times are based on the approximate amount of time required to assemble the recipe before baking or cooking. These times include preparation steps such as chopping; mixing; cooking rice, pasta, vegetables; etc. The fact that some preparation steps can be done simultaneously or during cooking is taken into account. The cook times are based on the minimum amount of time required to cook, bake or broil the food in the recipes.

Microwave Cooking Times: Microwave cooking times in this book are approximate. These recipes have been tested in 650- to 700-watt microwave ovens. Foods cooked in lower-wattage ovens may require longer cooking times. Use the cooking times as guidelines and check for doneness before adding more time.

ISBN 0-517-10337-0
Printed and bound in Canada

Campbell's

Quick and Easy
RECIPES

M'm! M'm! Good! cooking begins with Campbell's family of quality products. Inside this exciting new cookbook from Campbell, you're just minutes away from serving great-tasting, easy-to-prepare recipes the whole family will enjoy.

Quick and Easy Recipes features more than 150 delicious recipes using many of America's most popular brands: Campbell's condensed soups, V8 vegetable juice, Franco-American gravy, Prego spaghetti sauce, Campbell's tomato juice, Marie's salad dressing, and more. And, because your time spent in the kitchen is more valuable than ever, most of the recipes can be made from start to finish in *less than 30 minutes!*

We've included more than 200 beautiful color photographs, including many step-by-step technique pictures guaranteed to make cooking *easy and foolproof.* From taste-tempting appetizers, pizzas and desserts to savory main dishes, pasta and salads, you'll be a winner in a race against the clock with these *M'm! M'm! Good!* favorites from Campbell. From our Kitchens to yours — *ENJOY!*

Campbell's Family of Quality Products

$\mathscr{H}$ERB SEASONING GUIDE

Use this list of common cooking herbs as a guide for seasoning foods with herbs. Before you begin, here are a few tips for using fresh and dried herbs.

- Because dried herbs have a stronger flavor than fresh, substitute *three times* as much of a snipped fresh herb for the dried one. For example, use 1 tablespoon snipped *fresh* dill for 1 teaspoon *dried* dill weed.

- After measuring dried herb leaves, crush them before using to release their aromatic oils.

- When experimenting with an unfamiliar herb, use about 1/4 teaspoon dried herb for 4 servings, then taste before adding more.

Basil
- Large fragrant leaves with a sweet spicy taste — a cross between cloves and licorice.
- Available: fresh or dried leaves.
- Use to flavor meats, poultry, soups, stews and vegetables, especially tomatoes.

Bay Leaf
- Green, aromatic, shiny leaves with a pungent woodsy flavor.
- Available: fresh or dried whole leaves. The leaf should be removed before serving.
- Use to flavor meats, soups, stews and vegetables.

Chervil
- Small feathery leaves resembling parsley with a delicate anise-like flavor.
- Available: fresh or dried leaves.
- Use to flavor eggs, fish, poultry, salads and stuffing.

Chives
- Long tubular leaves with a mild onion flavor.
- Available: fresh or freeze-dried snipped leaves.
- Use to flavor cheese dishes, eggs, salads, sauces and vegetables.

Cilantro (also known as Chinese parsley)
- Delicate dark green leaves with a distinctive pungent flavor.
- Available: fresh or dried leaves.
- Used in Chinese, Indian and Mexican cuisines and to flavor meats, poultry and sauces.

Dill
- Thin feathery green and fragrant leaves with a delicate, distinctive flavor.
- Available: fresh or dried leaves (dried dill is known as dill weed) and in seeds.
- Use to flavor fish, pickles, poultry, salads, savory baked goods, vegetables and vinegars.

Marjoram
- Small silver-green leaves with a spicy sweet, mild oregano-like flavor.
- Available: fresh or dried leaves and ground.
- Use to flavor fish, poultry, eggs, sauces, soups and stews.

Mint
- The two most popular varieties are peppermint and spearmint. Peppermint has a strong, sweet cool flavor. Spearmint has a mild sweet flavor. Other mint varieties have fruity overtones such as apple, lemon, orange and pineapple.
- Available: fresh or dried leaves and in extract or oil forms.
- Use to flavor beverages, fruits, jellies, lamb, sauces and tomatoes.

Oregano
- Small green leaves with a strong, pungent slightly bitter flavor.
- Available: fresh or dried leaves and ground.
- Use sparingly to flavor pork, lamb, stews and vegetables.

Parsley
- Dark green leaves with a clean, fresh mild peppery flavor. The two most popular forms of parsley are curly-leaf or flat-leaf (Italian).
- Available: fresh or dehydrated leaves called parsley flakes.
- Use to flavor any dish except desserts.

Rosemary
- Resembling small pine needles, the silver-green needle-shaped leaves are aromatic with a pungent and piny sweet flavor.
- Available: fresh or dried leaves.
- Use to flavor dressings, lamb, poultry, stuffing and vegetables, especially potatoes.

Sage
- The oval, grey-green pebbly leaves have a pungent, slightly bitter flavor. Sage is the dominant flavoring used in most poultry stuffings.
- Available: fresh or dried leaves and rubbed or ground dried leaves.
- Use to flavor cheese, dressings, pork, sauces, sausages and stuffing.

Savory
- A member of the mint family there are two types of this strong-flavored herb: summer and winter. A cross between thyme and mint flavor, with a subtle spiciness, summer savory is the milder flavor of the two.
- Available: fresh or dried leaves and ground.
- Use to flavor bean or grain dishes, fish, meats and vegetables.

Tarragon
- Aromatic, slender dark green leaves with a distinctive licorice-like flavor.
- Available: fresh or dried leaves.
- Use to flavor dressings, eggs, fish, salads, sauces and vinegars.

Thyme
- Tiny, oval-shaped grey-green leaves with a spicy aroma and a strong, distinctive taste.
- Available: fresh or dried leaves and ground.
- Use to flavor cream sauces, dips, fish, poultry, meat and soups.

Campbell's

Quick and Easy
RECIPES

*K*ITCHEN ABC'S

See for yourself how easy it is to prepare delicious recipes from Campbell. Here we've illustrated some simple cooking techniques to help you take the guess-work out of recipe preparation and help you streamline your time and effort in the kitchen. You'll *see* the difference between chopping, cubing and mincing. You'll *see* how to measure ingredients the correct way. You'll *see* how to separate eggs, snip fresh herbs and much more.

To chop an onion quickly, halve it from top to root end. Place the onion halves flat side down; make parallel vertical slices. Then cut across the slices, as shown. This works well for other vegetables, too, such as potatoes.

Chopping refers to cutting a food into irregular pieces about the size of peas, as shown here with carrots.

Cubing refers to cutting a food into uniform pieces, usually about 1/2 inch on all sides, as shown here with green pepper.

Finely chopping or mincing refers to cutting a food into tiny irregular pieces, as shown here with garlic.

To mince fresh garlic, use a utility knife to cut peeled cloves into very tiny, irregular pieces.
To crush garlic, place a peeled clove in a garlic press and clamp the handles together. Always clean the garlic press thoroughly after each use.

To measure liquids, use a glass or clear plastic liquid measuring cup placed on a level surface. Bend down so your eye is level with the marking on the cup.

To measure flour, stir flour in canister to lighten it. Gently spoon the flour into a dry measuring cup; level off the top with straight edge of metal spatula or knife. When using measuring spoons for small amounts of dry ingredients (flour, sugar, cornstarch, for example) level off the spoon, as shown.

To measure brown sugar, spoon in sugar and press firmly in dry measuring cup so it holds the shape of the cup when it is turned out, as shown.

To measure shortening, press it firmly into a dry measuring cup or spoon with a rubber scraper, then level excess off with the straight edge of spatula or knife.

To measure margarine or butter, use the markings on the foil or paper wrapper as a guide. These markings indicate tablespoon and cup measures. If markings are not evident, measure margarine as you would shortening.

To separate eggs, gently crack the eggshell in the center with a knife as you hold the egg over a custard cup or bowl. Slide egg yolk back and forth from one shell half to the other, allowing the egg white to fall into the cup. Drop the yolk into another cup. TIP: It's easier to separate eggs while they're still cold.

Shredding means to cut a food into long, narrow strips, usually by rubbing it across a shredding surface. Use a shredder for cheese and vegetables. Some vegetables, such as lettuce or cabbage, can be shredded by thinly slicing with a knife.

Finely shredding means to rub a food across a fine shredding surface to form short, very narrow strips. This is usually done with lemon, orange and lime peel, and when very small pieces of other potent seasonings are needed.

Grating means to rub a food across a rough grating surface to make very fine particles. Grate hard cheeses such as Parmesan, and potent seasonings such as gingerroot.

Here's an easy way to marinate poultry and meat. Place the food in a plastic bag; set the bag in a deep bowl. Pour the marinade mixture over the food in the bag; close bag. Turn it to distribute the marinade evenly. Occasionally turn the bag during the marinating time so the marinade flavors all of the food.

To quickly snip fresh herbs, place the herb in a 1-cup glass measure and snip it with kitchen scissors. When substituting fresh herbs for dried, use three times more of the fresh herb. For example, use 1 tablespoon snipped fresh basil leaves instead of 1 teaspoon dried basil leaves.

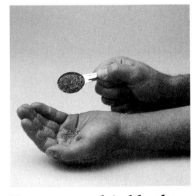

To measure dried herbs, lightly fill the appropriate measuring spoon to the top, keeping the herb as level with the top as possible. Then empty the spoon into your hand and crush the herb with your other hand. This breaks the leaves to better release their flavor.

$\mathcal{W}$EIGHTS & MEASURES

To shell shrimp, use your fingers to open the shell lengthwise down the body of the shrimp. Starting at the head end, peel back the shell and remove legs. If desired, gently pull on the tail portion of the shell and remove it.

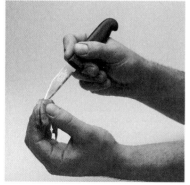

To devein shelled shrimp, use a small sharp knife to make a shallow slit along its back from the head end to the tail. Rinse under cold running water to remove the vein, using the tip of a knife, if necessary.

Solid Measurements

dash = pinch
generous dash = large pinch (about $1/16$ teaspoon)
3 teaspoons = 1 tablespoon
4 tablespoons = $1/4$ cup
5 $1/3$ tablespoons = $1/3$ cup
8 tablespoons = $1/2$ cup
10 $2/3$ tablespoons = $2/3$ cup
12 tablespoons = $3/4$ cup
16 tablespoons = 1 cup
1 ounce = 28.35 grams
1 pound = 450 grams
1 gram = 0.035 ounce
1 kilogram = 2.2 pounds

Liquid Measurements

1 tablespoon = $1/2$ fluid ounce
2 tablespoons = 1 fluid ounce
1 cup = 8 fluid ounces
1 cup = $1/2$ pint
2 cups = 1 pint = 16 fluid ounces
2 pints = 1 quart = 32 fluid ounces
4 quarts = 1 gallon = 128 fluid ounces
8 quarts = 1 peck
2 gallons = 1 peck
4 pecks = 1 bushel

Useful Equivalents

$1/8$ teaspoon = 0.5 milliliters (mL)
$1/4$ teaspoon = 1 milliliters (mL)
$1/2$ teaspoon = 2 milliliters (mL)
1 teaspoon = 5 milliliters (mL)
1 tablespoon = 15 milliliters (mL)
$1/4$ cup = 2 fluid ounces = 50 milliliters (mL)
$1/3$ cup = 3 fluid ounces = 75 milliliters (mL)
$1/2$ cup = 4 fluid ounces = 125 milliliters (mL)
1 cup = 8 fluid ounces = 250 milliliters (mL)
1 quart = 946.4 milliliters (mL)
1 liter = 1.06 quart

$\mathcal{F}$OOD EQUIVALENTS

Breads & Cookies		
	2 slices white bread	1 cup soft crumbs
	1 lb loaf white bread	14 to 20 slices
	14 square graham crackers	1 cup fine crumbs
	22 vanilla wafers	1 cup fine crumbs
	28 saltine crackers	1 cup fine crumbs

Dairy		
	1 lb margarine *or* butter	2 cups *or* 4 sticks
	¼-lb stick margarine *or* butter (1 stick)	8 tbsp
	1 cup heavy *or* whipping cream	2 cups whipped
	4-oz container whipped topping, thawed	1 ¾ cups
	8 oz cream cheese	1 cup
	1 lb Swiss *or* Cheddar cheese	4 cups shredded
	4 oz Parmesan *or* Romano cheese	1 ¼ cups grated
	1 large egg	3 tbsp beaten egg

Fruits		
	1 medium apple	about 1 cup sliced
	1 lb apples	3 medium
	1 medium banana	about ⅓ cup mashed
	1 lb bananas	3 medium
	1 pt blueberries	3 cups
	12-oz package whole cranberries	3 cups
	1 medium lemon	about 2 tbsp juice about 2 tsp shredded peel
	1 medium orange	⅓ to ½ cup juice
	1 large pineapple	about 4 cups cubed
	1 pt strawberries	about 3 ½ cups whole about 2 ¼ cups sliced

Noodles, Pasta & Rice		
	3 oz dry medium noodles (3 cups)	about 3 cups cooked
	8 oz dry elbow macaroni	about 4 cups cooked
	8 oz dry spaghetti	about 4 cups cooked
	1 cup uncooked regular long-grain rice	about 3 cups cooked
	1 cup uncooked quick-cooking rice	about 2 cups cooked

Vegetables		
	1 lb green beans, cut into 1-inch pieces	about 3 cups
	1 ½ lbs broccoli (1 large bunch)	about 5 cups flowerets
	1 small head cauliflower (1 ½ lbs)	about 4 cups flowerets
	1 lb cabbage	about 4 cups shredded
	1 medium carrot	about ½ cup shredded
	1 rib celery	about ½ cup sliced
	1 lb mushrooms	about 3 cups sliced
	4 oz snow peas	about 1 cup
	1 large green pepper	about 1 cup chopped
	1 lb all-purpose potatoes	3 medium
	1 medium green onion, sliced	about 2 tbsp
	1 lb yellow onions	5 to 6 medium
	1 lb tomatoes	3 medium

Miscellaneous		
	1 lb cooked boneless meat *or* poultry	3 cups diced
	1 lb raw boneless meat	2 cups cooked, cubed
	1 lb raw ground beef	2 ¾ cups cooked
	1 tbsp snipped fresh herbs	1 tsp dried leaves
	1 cup dried beans *or* peas	about 2 ¼ cups cooked

EMERGENCY SUBSTITUTIONS

When a recipe calls for:	You may substitute:
Bacon, cooked and crumbled, 1 slice	1 tablespoon bottled bacon pieces
Bread crumbs, dry, 1/4 cup	3/4 cup soft bread crumbs, 1/4 cup cracker crumbs, 1/4 cup cornflake crumbs or 2/3 cup rolled oats
Buttermilk, 1 cup	1 tablespoon lemon juice or vinegar plus enough milk to make 1 cup (Let stand 5 minutes before using.)
Chicken, cooked and cubed, 1 1/2 to 2 cups	2 cans (5 ounces each) Swanson premium chunk white chicken or turkey, drained
Cornstarch (for thickening), 1 tablespoon	2 tablespoons all-purpose flour or 2 teaspoons quick-cooking tapioca
Cream, heavy or whipping, 1 cup whipped and sweetened	2 cups thawed frozen whipped topping
Cream, sour, 1 cup	1 cup plain yogurt
Garlic, 1 clove	1/8 teaspoon garlic powder or minced dried garlic or 1/2 teaspoon bottled minced garlic
Ginger, fresh, minced, 1 tablespoon	1/4 teaspoon ground ginger
Half-and-half, 1 cup	2 tablespoons margarine or butter, melted, plus enough milk to make 1 cup
Herbs, fresh, snipped, 1 tablespoon	1 teaspoon dried herbs, crushed
Honey, 1/4 cup	1/4 cup light corn syrup
Margarine, 1 cup	1 cup butter or 1 cup vegetable shortening plus 1/4 teaspoon salt, if desired
Milk, fresh, whole, 1 cup	1 cup 2%, 1% or skim milk, or 1/2 cup evaporated milk plus 1/2 cup water
Mustard, prepared (in cooked mixtures), 1 tablespoon	1 teaspoon dry mustard
Mustard, prepared (as a spread/dip), 1 tablespoon	1/2 teaspoon dry mustard plus 2 teaspoons vinegar
Onion, 1 small, chopped (about 1/4 cup)	1 teaspoon onion powder or 1 tablespoon minced dried onion, rehydrated
Pepper, ground red (cayenne), 1/8 teaspoon	4 drops hot pepper sauce
Poultry seasoning, 1 teaspoon	3/4 teaspoon dried sage leaves, crushed, plus 1/4 teaspoon dried thyme leaves, crushed
Sugar, granulated, 1/2 cup	1/2 cup packed brown sugar
Zucchini, sliced, 1 cup	1 cup sliced summer squash

$\mathcal{N}$ACHOS

1 can (10 ³/₄ ounces) CAMPBELL'S condensed Cheddar Cheese Soup

¹/₂ cup salsa

1 bag (about 10 ounces) tortilla chips

VLASIC *or* EARLY CALIFORNIA Sliced Pitted Ripe Olives, chopped tomato, sliced green onions *and/or* chopped green or sweet red pepper

● In 1 ¹/₂-quart saucepan, combine soup and salsa. Over medium heat, heat through, stirring often.

● Arrange tortilla chips evenly on serving platter. Spoon sauce over chips. Top with olives, tomato, onions and/or chopped green or sweet red pepper.

TIP: To warm chips in the microwave oven, divide 1 bag (about 10 ounces) tortilla chips between 2 microwave-safe plates. Microwave 1 plate of chips at a time, uncovered, on HIGH 45 seconds.

Makes about 1 ¹/₂ cups or 6 appetizer servings.
Prep Time: 10 minutes
Cook Time: 5 minutes

$\mathcal{P}$IZZA FONDUE

1 jar (14 ounces) PREGO Pizza Sauce with Pepperoni Chunks

1 package (3 ounces) cream cheese, softened and cubed

Cubed Italian bread *and* tortilla chips for dipping

● In 2-quart saucepan over medium heat, heat pizza sauce until hot. Add cheese, a few cubes at a time, stirring after each addition until cheese is melted. *Do not boil.*

● Serve with cubed Italian bread or tortilla chips for dipping.

Makes about 1 ¹/₂ cups or 6 appetizer servings.
Prep Time: 5 minutes
Cook Time: 10 minutes

NACHOS

CURRIED CHICKEN SPREAD

3 tablespoons mayonnaise

3 tablespoons chopped chutney

1/4 teaspoon curry powder

1 can (5 ounces) SWANSON Premium
Chunk White Chicken, drained

1/2 cup chopped tart apple

1 tablespoon chopped dry roasted
peanuts

● In small bowl, combine mayonnaise,
chutney and curry powder. Stir in chicken,
apple and peanuts.

● Serve as a spread with crackers.

Makes about 1 cup or 8 appetizer servings.
Prep Time: 10 minutes

MEXICAN CHICKEN DIP

1/2 cup sour cream

1 tablespoon lime juice

1 teaspoon chili powder

1/2 teaspoon finely chopped, seeded
fresh jalapeño pepper

1/8 teaspoon garlic powder *or* 1 clove
garlic, minced

1 can (5 ounces) SWANSON Premium
Chunk White Chicken, drained

1 1/4 cups chopped seeded tomato
(about 1 large)

1/4 cup finely chopped green pepper

3 medium green onions, finely
chopped (about 1/4 cup)

Assorted PEPPERIDGE FARM Crackers
or tortilla chips for dipping

● In medium bowl, combine sour cream, lime
juice, chili powder, jalapeño pepper and
garlic powder. Stir in chicken, tomato, green
pepper and onions. Cover; refrigerate at least
2 hours before serving.

● Serve with crackers or tortilla chips for
dipping.

Makes about 2 cups or 8 appetizer servings.
Prep Time: 15 minutes
Chill Time: 2 hours

BROCCOLI-CHEESE DIP

1 can (10 ³/₄ ounces) CAMPBELL'S
condensed Broccoli Cheese Soup

1 package (10 ounces) frozen chopped
broccoli, thawed and drained

1 medium tomato, chopped
(about 1 cup)

¹/₂ cup sour cream

2 teaspoons Dijon-style mustard

Assorted PEPPERIDGE FARM Crackers
and fresh vegetables for dipping

● In medium bowl, combine soup, broccoli, tomato, sour cream and mustard. Cover; refrigerate at least 4 hours before serving.

● Serve with crackers and vegetables for dipping.

TIP: To quickly thaw a package of frozen chopped broccoli, use your microwave oven. Place frozen broccoli in a 1¹/₂-quart microwave-safe casserole. Cover with lid; microwave on HIGH 1 to 2 minutes or until broccoli can be easily separated. Drain the broccoli in a sieve and then you are ready to make this creamy dip.

Makes about 3 cups or 12 appetizer servings.
Prep Time: 10 minutes
Chill Time: 4 hours

MUSSELS MARINARA

3 pounds mussels

**1 ¹/₂ cups PREGO Marinara *or*
Traditional Spaghetti Sauce**

**¹/₃ cup Chablis *or* other dry white wine
(optional)**

Sliced Italian bread

Fresh tarragon sprigs for garnish

● Discard any mussels that remain open when tapped with fingers. Scrub mussels; trim "beards" with kitchen scissors, if necessary.

● In 4-quart saucepan over high heat, heat mussels, marinara sauce and wine to boiling. Reduce heat to low. Cover; cook 5 minutes or until mussels open, stirring occasionally. Discard any mussels that remain closed. Serve with bread. Garnish with tarragon, if desired.

Makes 8 appetizer servings.
Prep Time: 15 minutes
Cook Time: 15 minutes

MUSSELS MARINARA

1 Trim "beards" from mussels with kitchen scissors; discard.

2 Cook 5 minutes or until mussel shells open, stirring occasionally.

BACON BAGEL SNACKS

1 package (9 ounces) frozen plain mini bagels, split and toasted (10)

$^1/_2$ cup refrigerated MARIE'S Chunky Blue Cheese Dressing and Dip

6 slices bacon, cooked and crumbled

2 medium green onions, sliced (about $^1/_4$ cup)

● Spread each bagel half with about *1 teaspoon* dressing. Sprinkle with bacon and onion.

● On broiler pan or baking sheet, arrange bagel halves. Broil 5 inches from heat 2 minutes or until hot and bubbling. Serve immediately.

Makes 10 appetizer servings.
Prep Time: 20 minutes
Cook Time: 5 minutes

BUFFALO WINGS

12 chicken wings (about 2 pounds)

2 tablespoons hot pepper sauce

2 tablespoons margarine *or* butter

Celery sticks

Refrigerated MARIE'S Chunky Blue Cheese Dressing and Dip

● Cut wing tips off at joint and discard; cut each wing in half at joint.

● On rack in broiler pan, arrange wings. Broil 6 inches from heat 25 minutes or until chicken is no longer pink and juices run clear, turning occasionally. Transfer to serving platter.

● Meanwhile, in 1-quart saucepan over medium heat, heat hot pepper sauce and margarine until margarine is melted, stirring often. Drizzle over wings. Serve with celery sticks and dressing for dipping.

Makes 12 appetizer servings.
Prep Time: 10 minutes
Cook Time: 25 minutes

BACON BAGEL SNACKS (TOP)
BUFFALO WINGS (BOTTOM)

ORANGE MIST

1 can (46 ounces) V8 Vegetable Juice

1 can (6 ounces) frozen orange juice concentrate

1 ½ cups seltzer water *or* orange-flavored seltzer water

● In large pitcher, combine "V8" juice and orange juice.

● Stir in seltzer water. Pour immediately over ice.

Makes about 7 ½ cups or 10 servings.
Prep Time: 5 minutes

FRUIT WARMER

1 can (46 ounces) V8 Vegetable Juice

4 cups apple cider

2 cups brewed tea

1 ½ cups apricot nectar

⅓ cup packed brown sugar

● In 6-quart Dutch oven, combine "V8" juice, cider, tea, apricot nectar and sugar. Over high heat, heat to boiling. Reduce heat to low. Cover; heat 10 minutes.

● Ladle into mugs.

Makes about 13 cups or 16 servings.
Prep Time: 10 minutes
Cook Time: 20 minutes

SPICY HOT REFRESHER

1 ½ cups SPICY HOT V8 Vegetable Juice

½ cup chopped, seeded, peeled cucumber

1 tablespoon lime juice

¼ teaspoon chili powder

1 cup ice cubes

Cucumber slices for garnish

● In covered blender or food processor, combine "V8" juice, chopped cucumber, lime juice and chili powder. Blend until smooth. Add ice cubes, one at a time, blending until ice is finely crushed.

● Serve immediately. Garnish with cucumber slices, if desired.

Makes about 2 ½ cups or 4 servings.
Prep Time: 10 minutes

LIGHT 'N TANGY TWISTER

2 cups LIGHT 'N TANGY V8 Vegetable Juice

$^1/_3$ cup orange juice

$^1/_4$ cup grapefruit juice

2 teaspoons honey

Orange slices for garnish

● In pitcher, combine "V8" juice, orange juice, grapefruit juice and honey.

● Pour over ice. Garnish with orange slices, if desired.

Makes about 2 $^1/_2$ cups or 3 servings.
Prep Time: 5 minutes

BLOODY EIGHT

3 cups V8 Vegetable Juice

1 teaspoon prepared horseradish

1 teaspoon Worcestershire sauce

1/2 teaspoon hot pepper sauce

Lemon slices for garnish

● In pitcher, combine "V8" juice, horseradish, Worcestershire sauce and hot pepper sauce.

● Pour over ice. Garnish with lemon slices, if desired.

TIP: For more flavor, increase prepared horseradish to 1 tablespoon.

Makes about 3 cups or 4 servings.
Prep Time: 5 minutes

TROPICAL SLUSH

3/4 cup V8 Vegetable Juice

3/4 cup pineapple juice

1/2 cup diced canned peaches

Dash ground ginger

1 cup ice cubes

● In covered blender or food processor, combine "V8" juice, pineapple juice, peaches and ginger. Blend until smooth. Add ice cubes, one at a time, blending until ice is finely crushed.

● Serve immediately.

Papaya Slush: Prepare Tropical Slush as directed above, *except* substitute 1/2 cup diced *ripe papaya* for the peaches.

Makes about 3 cups or 4 servings.
Prep Time: 10 minutes

SUNSHINE PUNCH

3 cups V8 Vegetable Juice

1/2 cup orange juice

1/2 cup unsweetened pineapple juice

1 tablespoon honey

1/8 teaspoon ground ginger

1 cup tonic water

Orange slices for garnish

● In pitcher, combine "V8" juice, orange juice, pineapple juice, honey and ginger. Cover; chill at least 2 hours before serving.

● Stir in tonic. Pour immediately over ice. Garnish with orange slices, if desired.

Makes about 5 cups or 10 servings.
Prep Time: 5 minutes
Chill Time: 2 hours

$\mathcal{F}$ROSTY GAZPACHO

1 can (5.5 ounces) V8 Vegetable Juice

$^1/_2$ cup chopped, peeled, seeded cucumber

$^1/_4$ cup chopped green pepper

$^1/_2$ teaspoon Worcestershire sauce

$^1/_4$ teaspoon onion powder

Generous dash hot pepper sauce

1 cup ice cubes

Cucumber spears for garnish

● In covered blender or food processor, combine "V8" juice, chopped cucumber, green pepper, Worcestershire sauce, onion powder and hot pepper sauce. Blend until smooth. Add ice cubes, one at a time, blending until ice is finely crushed.

● Serve immediately. Garnish with cucumber spears, if desired.

Makes about 2 $^1/_2$ cups or 4 servings.
Prep Time: 10 minutes

$\mathcal{T}$ANGY MULLED CIDER

4 whole cloves

1 medium apple, cored and cut into 4 wedges

6 cups LIGHT 'N TANGY V8 Vegetable Juice

2 cups apple cider

1 cinnamon stick (3 inches)

● Insert 1 clove into each apple wedge.

● In 3-quart saucepan, combine "V8" juice, cider, cinnamon stick and apple. Over medium heat, heat 15 minutes. Discard apple and cinnamon stick. Ladle into mugs.

TIP: Spiced cider can be placed in crockpot to keep warm.

Makes about 8 cups or 10 servings.
Prep Time: 5 minutes
Cook Time: 15 minutes

$\mathcal{C}$RANBERRY SIPPER

3 cups V8 Vegetable Juice

1 cup cranberry juice

1/8 teaspoon ground cinnamon

Cinnamon sticks for garnish

● In 2-quart saucepan, combine "V8" juice, cranberry juice and cinnamon. Over high heat, heat to boiling, stirring occasionally.

● Ladle into mugs. Garnish with cinnamon sticks, if desired.

Makes about 4 cups or 6 servings.
Prep Time: 5 minutes
Cook Time: 5 minutes

CHOCOLATE-BANANA CREAM PIE

1 package (9 ounces) ready-made graham cracker crust (about 9 inches)

2 medium bananas, sliced

1 jar (13 ounces) MARIE'S Creamy Glaze for Bananas

1 package (about 4 ounces) chocolate instant pudding mix

Thawed frozen whipped topping *or* whipped heavy cream

Banana slices, strawberry slices *and* grated semisweet chocolate for garnish

● In crust in single layer, arrange the 2 sliced bananas. Spoon glaze over bananas, spreading to cover.

● Prepare pudding according to package directions for pie filling. Pour pudding over banana mixture.

● Cover; refrigerate at least 2 hours before serving. Pipe or spoon whipped topping around edge and in center of pie. Garnish with additional banana slices, strawberry slices and grated chocolate, if desired.

Makes 6 servings.
Prep Time: 15 minutes
Chill Time: 2 hours

BLUEBERRY-CRUNCH PARFAITS

1 cup MARIE'S Glaze for Blueberries

1 cup fresh *or* frozen blueberries

2 cups vanilla-flavored yogurt

1/2 cup granola

Kiwi fruit slices *and* shredded lemon peel for garnish

● In small bowl, combine glaze and blueberries. In 4 parfait glasses, layer *half* of the yogurt, *half* of the blueberry mixture and *half* of the granola. Repeat layers. Garnish with kiwi slices and lemon peel, if desired.

TIP: Depending on the height of your parfait glasses, use a long-handled spoon (iced-tea spoon) to neatly add each ingredient layer. Use a separate spoon for each layer to keep from mixing the ingredients.

Makes 4 servings.
Prep Time: 10 minutes

CHOCOLATE-BANANA CREAM PIE (TOP)
BLUEBERRY-CRUNCH PARFAITS (MIDDLE)

POPPY SEED FRUIT DIP

½ cup refrigerated MARIE'S Poppy
  Seed Dressing and Dip

2 tablespoons sugar

1 teaspoon vanilla extract

2 cups whipped heavy cream *or* thawed
  frozen whipped topping

Grated semisweet chocolate for garnish

Assorted fresh fruit for dipping

● In medium bowl, combine dressing, sugar and vanilla. Gently fold in whipped cream.

● Garnish with chocolate, if desired. Serve with fruit for dipping.

TIP: Serve as a topping for fresh fruit, pound cake, brownies, banana bread or spice cake.

Makes about 2 cups or 8 servings.
Prep Time: 15 minutes

❶ Gently fold whipped cream into dressing mixture.

❷ Scoop out balls of cantaloupe using a melon baller or a 1 teaspoon measuring spoon.

❸ Slice off bottom and top of fresh pineapple.

POPPY SEED FRUIT DIP

4 Stand pineapple on a cut end. Cut off wide strips of peel, from top to bottom.

5 Remove "eyes" using a curved, serrated citrus knife, the point of sharp paring knife or vegetable peeler.

6 Halve the pineapple lengthwise; cut halves lengthwise into quarters. Cut hard center core from quarters; discard cores. Cut pineapple into spears, then into bite-size pieces.

APPLES 'N' CINNAMON TOPPING

1 cup MARIE'S Glaze for Strawberries

1/2 cup water

1/4 cup sugar

1/4 teaspoon ground cinnamon

3 medium cooking apples, *each* cored, peeled and cut into 8 wedges (about 3 cups)

● In 10-inch skillet, combine glaze, water, sugar and cinnamon. Over medium heat, heat to boiling, stirring constantly.

● Add apples; heat to boiling. Reduce heat to low. Cook 10 minutes or until apples are tender, spooning glaze over apples occasionally. Transfer to bowl. Cover; refrigerate at least 4 hours before serving.

● Use as a side dish or dessert. Also can be used as a fruit topping for pancakes and waffles.

Makes 6 servings.
Prep Time: 10 minutes
Cook Time: 20 minutes
Chill Time: 4 hours

CLASSIC TOMATO SOUP-SPICE CAKE

2 cups all-purpose flour

1 1/3 cups sugar

4 teaspoons baking powder

1 1/2 teaspoons ground allspice

1 teaspoon baking soda

1 teaspoon ground cinnamon

1/2 teaspoon ground cloves

1 can (10 3/4 ounces) CAMPBELL'S condensed Tomato Soup

1/2 cup vegetable shortening

2 eggs

1/4 cup water

Cream cheese frosting *or* butter cream frosting

● Preheat oven to 350°F. Grease and flour two 8-inch round cake pans.

● In large bowl, combine flour, sugar, baking powder, allspice, baking soda, cinnamon, cloves, soup, shortening, eggs and water. With mixer at low speed, beat until well mixed, constantly scraping bowl with rubber spatula. At high speed, beat 4 minutes, occasionally scraping bowl. Pour batter into prepared pans.

● Bake 35 to 40 minutes or until toothpick inserted in center comes out clean. Cool in pans on wire racks 10 minutes. Carefully remove from pans; cool completely. Frost with cream cheese frosting, if desired.

Makes 8 servings.
Prep Time: 10 minutes
Bake and Cool Time: 3 hours

BLUEBERRY-PEACH SUNDAES

³/₄ cup MARIE'S Glaze for Peaches

¹/₄ teaspoon almond extract

2 cups vanilla nonfat frozen yogurt

**2 cups sliced fresh nectarines *or*
peaches (about 2 medium)**

1 cup fresh blueberries

Fresh mint sprigs for garnish

● In small bowl, combine glaze and extract; set aside.

● In 6 dessert dishes, spoon 1/3 cup yogurt. Divide nectarines and blueberries among dishes. Spoon 2 tablespoons glaze mixture over fruit and yogurt. Garnish with mint, if desired. Serve immediately.

TIP: You may substitute frozen, sliced peaches and frozen blueberries, thawed and drained, for the fresh fruit.

Makes 6 servings.
Prep Time: 10 minutes

STRAWBERRY ANGEL DESSERT

1 package (about 14 ounces) angel food cake mix

4 cups sliced fresh strawberries (about 1 quart)

1 container (14 ounces) MARIE'S Glaze for Strawberries

1 1/2 teaspoons lemon juice

3/4 cup thawed frozen whipped topping *or* whipped heavy cream

● Prepare cake according to package directions. Meanwhile, in medium bowl, combine strawberries, glaze and lemon juice.

● With serrated knife, cut cake in *half* horizontally, making two layers. Spoon *two-thirds* of strawberry mixture on bottom cake layer. Top with remaining layer; spoon remaining strawberry mixture on top. Serve with whipped topping.

TIP: Prepare Strawberry Angel Dessert as directed above, *except* substitute 8-inch ready-made angel food cake for the mix and *reduce* strawberries to 2 cups, strawberry glaze to 3/4 cup and lemon juice to 1/2 teaspoon.

Makes 12 servings.
Prep Time: 30 minutes
Bake and Cool Time: 3 hours

BANANA SPLIT CAKE

24 PEPPERIDGE FARM Bordeaux Cookies, broken

2 medium bananas, thinly sliced

1 jar (13 ounces) MARIE'S Creamy Glaze for Bananas

1 container (8 ounces) frozen whipped topping, thawed (3 cups) *or* whipped heavy cream

2 tablespoons chocolate syrup

1/4 cup chopped peanuts

● In 2-quart casserole, arrange in single layer, *half* of the cookies, *half* of the bananas, *half* of the glaze and *half* of the whipped topping. Repeat layers.

● Drizzle chocolate syrup over topping. Cover; refrigerate at least 4 hours or overnight before serving. Just before serving, sprinkle with peanuts.

TIP: You may substitute *24 chocolate wafers or 30 vanilla wafers* for the Bordeaux cookies.

Makes 8 servings.
Prep Time: 10 minutes
Chill Time: 4 hours

BANANA SPLIT CAKE

❶ Arrange *half* of the banana slices over cookies.

❷ Spoon *half* of the glaze over bananas.

❸ Drizzle chocolate syrup over whipped topping.

*H*OT TURKEY SANDWICHES

2 tablespoons margarine *or* butter

2 small carrots, thinly sliced diagonally
(about $^1/_2$ cup)

1 medium onion, chopped
(about $^1/_2$ cup)

$^1/_4$ cup sliced celery

$^3/_4$ teaspoon snipped fresh thyme
leaves *or* $^1/_4$ teaspoon dried thyme
leaves, crushed (optional)

1 can (10 $^1/_2$ ounces)
FRANCO-AMERICAN Turkey Gravy

Sliced cooked turkey (about $^1/_2$ pound)

4 diagonally sliced pieces Italian bread

● In 2-quart saucepan over medium heat, in hot margarine, cook carrots, onion, celery and thyme until vegetables are tender, stirring occasionally.

● Stir in gravy. Heat to boiling. Add turkey. Heat through, stirring occasionally. Divide turkey and gravy mixture evenly among bread slices.

Serving Suggestion: Hot Turkey Sandwiches are served with steamed broccoli flowerets.

Makes 4 servings.
Prep Time: 10 minutes
Cook Time: 10 minutes

*S*OUPERBURGER SANDWICHES

1 pound ground beef

1 medium onion, chopped
(about $^1/_2$ cup)

1 can (10 $^3/_4$ ounces) CAMPBELL'S
condensed Cheddar Cheese Soup

2 tablespoons ketchup

$^1/_8$ teaspoon pepper

6 hamburger buns, split and toasted

● In 10-inch skillet over medium-high heat, cook beef and onion until beef is browned and onion is tender, stirring to separate meat. Spoon off fat.

● Stir in soup, ketchup and pepper. Reduce heat to low. Heat through, stirring occasionally. Serve on buns.

Makes about 3 cups or 6 servings.
Prep Time: 5 minutes
Cook Time: 15 minutes

HOT TURKEY SANDWICHES

*J*TALIAN SAUSAGE SANDWICHES

1 pound sweet Italian pork sausage, casing removed

1 medium green pepper, cut into strips (about 1 cup)

1 medium onion, sliced and separated into rings (about ¹/₂ cup)

1 ¹/₂ cups CAMPBELL'S Italian Style Spaghetti Sauce

4 hard rolls (*each* about 6 inches long), split lengthwise

● In 10-inch skillet over medium-high heat, cook sausage, green pepper and onion until sausage is browned and no longer pink, stirring to separate meat. Spoon off fat.

● Stir in spaghetti sauce. Heat to boiling. Reduce heat to low. Cover; cook 5 minutes, stirring occasionally. Spoon mixture into rolls.

Serving Suggestion: Italian Sausage Sandwiches are served with carrot and celery sticks, cherry pepper and pimento-stuffed olives.

Makes about 3 cups or 4 servings.
Prep Time: 15 minutes
Cook Time: 20 minutes

BARBECUE BURGERS

1 pound ground beef

1 teaspoon cornstarch

1 cup CAMPBELL'S Tomato Juice

1 tablespoon packed brown sugar

1 tablespoon Worcestershire sauce

1 teaspoon prepared mustard

$^1/_8$ teaspoon garlic powder

1 medium onion, sliced and separated into rings (about $^1/_2$ cup)

2 hamburger buns *or* English muffins, split and toasted

● Shape beef into four 4-inch round patties.

● In 10-inch skillet over medium-high heat, cook patties 5 minutes or until browned, turning once. Remove; set aside. Pour off fat.

● Meanwhile, in small bowl, stir together cornstarch, tomato juice, brown sugar, Worcestershire sauce, mustard and garlic until smooth. Add to skillet. Cook until mixture boils and thickens, stirring constantly.

● Add onion. Return patties to skillet. Reduce heat to low. Cover; cook 5 minutes, stirring occasionally. Serve patties open-face on buns. Spoon sauce over patties.

Serving Suggestion: Barbecue Burgers are served on romaine lettuce and accompanied with carrot sticks and pickle slices. Garnish with celery leaves.

Makes 4 servings.
Prep Time: 10 minutes
Cook Time: 15 minutes

Shortcut Sloppy Joes

1 pound ground beef

1 can (11 $^1/_8$ ounces) CAMPBELL'S
condensed Italian Tomato Soup

$^1/_4$ cup water

2 teaspoons Worcestershire sauce

$^1/_8$ teaspoon pepper

6 Kaiser rolls *or* hamburger buns, split
and toasted

- In 10-inch skillet over medium-high heat, cook beef until browned, stirring to separate meat. Spoon off fat.

- Stir in soup, water, Worcestershire sauce and pepper. Heat through, stirring occasionally. Serve on rolls.

Souper Joes: Prepare Shortcut Sloppy Joes as directed above, *except* substitute 1 pound *bulk pork sausage* for the ground beef, add 1 small *green pepper*, chopped (about $^1/_2$ cup), with the sausage and omit water, Worcestershire sauce and pepper. Serve on 4 *hard rolls* (*each* about 7 inches long), split and toasted.

Makes about 3 cups or 6 servings.
Prep Time: 5 minutes
Cook Time: 15 minutes

Chicken Quesadillas

1 can (10 $^3/_4$ ounces) CAMPBELL'S
condensed Cream of Chicken Soup

2 cans (5 ounces each) SWANSON
Premium Chunk White Chicken,
drained

1 cup shredded Cheddar cheese
(4 ounces)

1 fresh *or* canned jalapeño pepper,
seeded and finely chopped
(about 1 tablespoon), optional

8 flour tortillas (8 inches *each*)

Salsa

Sour cream

Fresh green onions, jalapeño pepper
slices *and* fresh cilantro sprigs for
garnish

- In small bowl, combine soup, chicken, $^1/_2$ cup Cheddar cheese and chopped jalapeño pepper.

- Top *half* of each tortilla with $^1/_4$ cup soup mixture, spreading evenly to within $^1/_2$ inch of edge. Moisten edges of tortillas with water; fold over, pressing edges to seal. On 2 large baking sheets, arrange filled tortillas.

- Bake at 400°F. for 8 minutes or until hot. Sprinkle with remaining $^1/_2$ cup Cheddar cheese. Serve with salsa and sour cream. Garnish with green onions, jalapeño pepper and cilantro, if desired.

Makes 8 quesadillas or 4 servings.
Prep Time: 15 minutes
Cook Time: 10 minutes

CHICKEN QUESADILLAS

1 In bowl, combine soup, chicken, *¹/₂ cup* Cheddar cheese and chopped jalapeño pepper.

2 Top *half* of each tortilla with *¹/₄ cup* soup mixture.

3 Fold over tortilla, pressing edges to seal.

CHICKEN SALAD SANDWICHES

1 can (5 ounces) SWANSON Premium Chunk White Chicken, drained

¹/₄ cup chopped celery

3 tablespoons mayonnaise

1 tablespoon finely chopped onion

1 teaspoon lemon juice

Dash pepper

Lettuce leaves

Tomato slices

4 slices bread, toasted

● In small bowl, combine chicken, celery, mayonnaise, onion, lemon juice and pepper.

● Arrange lettuce leaves and tomato slices on *2 bread slices*. Top with chicken mixture and remaining *2 bread slices*.

Makes 2 servings.
Prep Time: 10 minutes

BARBECUED CHICKEN SANDWICHES

1 tablespoon margarine *or* butter

1 small green pepper, chopped (about ¹/₂ cup), optional

¹/₄ cup chopped celery

1 small onion, chopped (about ¹/₄ cup)

2 cans (5 ounces *each*) SWANSON Premium Chunk White Chicken, drained

¹/₂ cup bottled barbecue sauce

4 hamburger buns, split and toasted

● In 2-quart saucepan over medium heat, in hot margarine, cook green pepper, celery and onion until tender. Add chicken and barbecue sauce. Heat through, stirring occasionally.

● Divide chicken mixture evenly among buns.

Makes 4 servings.
Prep Time: 10 minutes
Cook Time: 10 minutes

CHICKEN PIZZA MUFFINS

4 English muffins, split and toasted

1/2 cup PREGO Pizza Sauce – Traditional Variety

2 cans (5 ounces *each*) SWANSON Premium Chunk White Chicken, drained

1 cup shredded mozzarella cheese (4 ounces)

Crushed red pepper, dried oregano leaves *or* garlic powder (optional)

● Arrange muffins on broiler pan. Spread each muffin half with *1 tablespoon* pizza sauce. Divide chicken and cheese evenly among muffin halves. Sprinkle with red pepper.

● Broil 4 inches from heat 3 minutes or until cheese is melted.

Serving Suggestion: Chicken Pizza Muffins are served with pitted ripe olives, green onions, radishes and pepperoncini salad peppers.

Makes 8 pizzas or 4 servings.
Prep Time: 10 minutes
Cook Time: 5 minutes

WHITE PIZZA MUFFINS

$^1/_2$ cup refrigerated MARIE'S Creamy Ranch Dressing and Dip

1 medium tomato, chopped (about 1 cup)

6 English muffins, split and toasted

2 medium green onions, chopped (about $^1/_4$ cup)

1 cup shredded Monterey Jack cheese (4 ounces)

● In small bowl, combine dressing and tomato. Spread each muffin half with about *1 tablespoon* dressing mixture. Top with onion; sprinkle with cheese.

● On baking sheet, arrange muffin halves. Bake at 400°F. for 8 minutes or until hot and cheese is melted. Serve immediately.

Makes 12 pizzas or 6 servings.
Prep Time: 15 minutes
Cook Time: 10 minutes

DEEP-DISH PIZZA

1 package (10 ounces) refrigerated pizza crust dough

$^3/_4$ cup PREGO Pizza Sauce with Pepperoni Chunks

1 $^1/_2$ cups shredded mozzarella cheese (6 ounces)

Cherry tomatoes *and* fresh parsley for garnish

● Preheat oven to 425°F. Grease 10-inch ovenproof skillet.

● Unroll dough and pat onto bottom and 1 1/2 inches up side of skillet. With fork, prick dough thoroughly. Bake 12 minutes or until crust is set and just begins to brown. Gently lift and slide the partially-baked crust onto baking sheet.

● Spread pizza sauce over crust. Sprinkle with cheese. Bake 10 minutes or until cheese is melted and crust is golden. Let stand 5 minutes. Cut into wedges. If you like, for easier serving, return pizza to skillet. Garnish with tomatoes and parsley, if desired.

Makes 4 servings.
Prep Time: 10 minutes
Cook Time: 25 minutes
Stand Time: 5 minutes

DEEP-DISH PIZZA

1 Unroll pizza crust dough and pat onto bottom and 1 ½ inches up side of 10-inch skillet.

2 Carefully remove the baked crust from skillet.

3 Spread pizza sauce over baked crust.

CALIFORNIA PIZZA BREADS

1 loaf (about 1 pound) Italian bread (about 15 inches long), cut in half lengthwise

1/3 cup refrigerated MARIE'S Creamy Italian Garlic Dressing and Dip

1 cup diced sweet red, green *and* yellow peppers

1 can (2 1/4 ounces) VLASIC *or* EARLY CALIFORNIA Sliced Ripe Olives, drained

2 medium green onions, sliced (about 1/4 cup)

3/4 cup shredded mozzarella cheese (3 ounces)

● On baking sheet, arrange bread cut-side up. Bake at 425°F. for 5 minutes or until lightly toasted. Cut bread in half to make 4 pizza breads.

● Spread each pizza bread half with some dressing. Top with red, green and yellow peppers, olives and onions. Sprinkle with cheese.

● Bake 10 minutes or until hot and cheese is melted.

Makes 4 servings.
Prep Time: 15 minutes
Cook Time: 15 minutes

GARDEN PITA PIZZAS

3 whole wheat pita breads (6-inch rounds)

1 tablespoon olive *or* vegetable oil

1 1/2 cups fresh broccoli flowerets

3 medium carrots, thinly sliced (about 1 cup)

1 large green pepper, chopped (about 1 cup)

1 medium green onion, chopped (about 2 tablespoons)

1 cup PREGO Pizza Sauce with Sliced Mushrooms

1 cup shredded mozzarella cheese (4 ounces)

● Split each pita bread into two flat rounds, making a total of 6 rounds. Place on 2 baking sheets. Bake at 400°F. for 5 minutes or until lightly toasted.

● In 10-inch skillet over medium heat, in hot oil, cook broccoli, carrots, green pepper and onion until vegetables are tender-crisp, stirring often. Set aside.

● Spread each pita round with *2 heaping tablespoons* pizza sauce. Divide vegetable mixture and cheese evenly among pitas. Bake 5 minutes or until cheese is melted.

Serving Suggestion: California Pizza Breads (top) are served on leaf lettuce. Garnish with tomato wedges, pimento-stuffed olives and fresh parsley. Garden Pita Pizzas (bottom) are served with romaine lettuce, pickle slices, halved cherry pepper and fresh parsley.

Makes 6 pizzas or 6 servings.
Prep Time: 15 minutes
Cook Time: 15 minutes

CALIFORNIA PIZZA BREADS (TOP)
GARDEN PITA PIZZAS (BOTTOM)

$\mathcal{S}$OUPER SAUSAGE CORN BREAD

1 can (10 $^3/_4$ ounces) CAMPBELL'S condensed Golden Corn Soup

2 eggs

$^1/_4$ cup milk

1 package (12 to 14 ounces) corn muffin mix

$^1/_4$ pound bulk pork sausage, crumbled, cooked and drained

● Preheat oven to 400°F. Grease 9-inch square baking pan; set aside.

● In medium bowl, combine soup, eggs and milk. Stir in corn muffin mix just until blended. Gently fold in sausage.

● Spoon corn muffin mixture into prepared pan, spreading evenly. Bake 20 minutes or until lightly browned and toothpick inserted in center comes out clean. Cool on wire rack 10 minutes before cutting into squares. Serve warm.

Makes about 9 servings.
Prep Time: 10 minutes
Cook Time: 20 minutes

$\mathcal{P}$ARMESAN BREAD DELUXE

1 loaf (about 1 pound) Italian bread

$^1/_2$ cup refrigerated MARIE'S Creamy Caesar Dressing and Dip

$^1/_3$ cup grated Parmesan cheese

3 tablespoons finely chopped green onions

● Cut 24 ($^1/_2$ inch thick) slices from bread. (Reserve remaining bread for other use.)

● In small bowl, combine dressing, cheese and onion. Spread generous teaspoon of dressing mixture onto each bread slice.

● On baking sheet arrange bread slices. Broil, 4 inches from heat, 1 minute or until golden brown. Serve warm.

Makes 24 slices or 12 servings.
Prep Time: 10 minutes
Cook Time: 5 minutes

CARROT-SPICE MUFFINS

2 cups all-purpose flour

3/4 cup sugar

2 teaspoons baking powder

1 teaspoon ground cinnamon

1/2 teaspoon salt

1/4 teaspoon baking soda

1/4 teaspoon ground ginger

1/4 teaspoon ground nutmeg

1 cup CAMPBELL'S Tomato Juice

1/2 cup chopped walnuts *or* raisins

1/2 cup shredded carrot (about 1 medium carrot)

1/3 cup vegetable oil

1 egg

● Preheat oven to 400°F. Grease twelve 2 1/2-inch muffin cups or line with paper bake cups; set aside.

● In large bowl, combine flour, sugar, baking powder, cinnamon, salt, baking soda, ginger and nutmeg; set aside.

● In medium bowl, combine tomato juice, walnuts, carrot, oil and egg. Add egg mixture to flour mixture. Stir just until moistened (batter should be lumpy). Spoon into prepared muffin cups.

● Bake 25 minutes or until toothpick inserted in center comes out clean. Immediately remove from pan. Serve warm.

TIP: If muffins can't be served at once, loosen baked muffins from the pan and tip each muffin to one side in the pan. This will keep them from steaming and becoming soggy on the bottom.

Makes 12 muffins.
Prep Time: 15 minutes
Cook Time: 25 minutes

CHICKEN DIJON

2 tablespoons margarine *or* butter

4 skinless, boneless chicken breast halves (about 1 pound)

1 medium onion, chopped (about 1/2 cup)

1 can (10 3/4 ounces) CAMPBELL'S condensed Cream of Mushroom Soup

1/4 cup apple juice *or* milk

1 tablespoon chopped fresh parsley *or* dried parsley flakes

1 tablespoon Dijon-style mustard

4 cups hot cooked medium egg noodles (about 4 cups dry)

● In 10-inch skillet over medium-high heat, in *1 tablespoon* hot margarine, cook chicken 10 minutes or until browned on both sides. Remove; set aside.

● Reduce heat to medium. In same skillet, in remaining *1 tablespoon* hot margarine, cook onion until tender, stirring often.

● Stir in soup, apple juice, parsley and mustard. Heat to boiling. Return chicken to skillet. Reduce heat to low. Cover; cook 5 minutes or until chicken is no longer pink, stirring occasionally. Serve with noodles. Garnish with parsley and apples, if desired.

Makes 4 servings.
Prep Time: 5 minutes
Cook Time: 25 minutes

TIP: The U.S. Department of Agriculture operates a toll-free Meat and Poultry Hot Line to answer your food safety questions about meat and poultry. From 10 a.m. to 4 p.m. Eastern Standard Time, Monday through Friday, home economists will answer your meat and poultry questions--just dial 1-800-535-4555. If you are in Washington, DC, metropolitan area, dial (202) 447-3333.*

*Source: U.S. Department of Agriculture-Food Safety and Inspection Service.

CHICKEN PARMESAN

1 egg *or* 2 egg whites, beaten

4 skinless, boneless chicken breast halves (about 1 pound)

$^1/_2$ cup Italian-seasoned dry bread crumbs

2 tablespoons margarine *or* butter

2 cups PREGO Traditional Spaghetti Sauce

$^1/_2$ cup shredded mozzarella cheese (2 ounces)

1 tablespoon grated Parmesan cheese

1 tablespoon snipped fresh parsley *or* 1 teaspoon dried parsley flakes

4 cups hot cooked spaghetti (about 8 ounces dry)

● Dip chicken into egg. On waxed paper, coat chicken with crumbs. In 10-inch skillet over medium heat, in hot margarine, cook chicken 10 minutes or until browned on both sides. Remove; set aside.

● In same skillet, heat spaghetti sauce to boiling. Add chicken. Reduce heat to low. Cover; cook 5 minutes or until chicken is no longer pink. Sprinkle with cheeses and parsley. Cover; cook until cheese is melted. Serve with spaghetti.

Makes 4 servings.
Prep Time: 5 minutes
Cook Time: 25 minutes

CHICKEN EL PASO

1/2 **cup dry bread crumbs**

1/2 **teaspoon chili powder**

4 **skinless, boneless chicken breast halves (about 1 pound)**

1/4 **cup refrigerated MARIE'S Creamy Ranch Dressing and Dip**

Salsa

● On waxed paper, combine crumbs and chili powder. In shallow dish, dip chicken into dressing. Coat with crumb mixture.

● On baking sheet, arrange chicken. Bake at 400°F. for 20 minutes or until chicken is no longer pink, turning once during baking. Serve with salsa.

Makes 4 servings.
Prep Time: 5 minutes
Cook Time: 20 minutes

SANTA FE CHILI CHICKEN

1 **tablespoon all-purpose flour**

1 **tablespoon chili powder**

4 **skinless, boneless chicken breast halves (about 1 pound)**

1 **tablespoon vegetable oil**

1 **can (10** 1/2 **ounces) FRANCO-AMERICAN Chicken Gravy**

1/4 **cup shredded Monterey Jack cheese (1 ounce)**

4 **warm flour tortillas (8 inches** *each*)**, quartered (optional)**

VLASIC Pepperoncini Salad Peppers *and* **cherry tomatoes for garnish**

● On waxed paper, combine flour and chili powder. Coat chicken with flour mixture.

● In 10-inch skillet over medium heat, in hot oil, cook chicken 10 minutes or until browned on both sides. Remove; set aside. Pour off fat.

● In same skillet, heat gravy to boiling. Return chicken to skillet. Reduce heat to low. Cover; cook 5 minutes or until chicken is no longer pink, stirring occasionally. Sprinkle with cheese and additional *chili powder.* Serve with tortillas. Garnish with salad peppers and tomatoes, if desired.

Makes 4 servings.
Prep Time: 10 minutes
Cook Time: 15 minutes

SANTA FE CHILI CHICKEN

1 Coat chicken with flour mixture.

2 In same skillet, heat gravy to boiling. Return chicken to skillet.

𝒯ANGY BROILED CHICKEN

6 skinless, boneless chicken breast halves (about 1 ¹/₂ pounds)

1 cup refrigerated MARIE'S ZESTY Fat Free Red Wine Vinaigrette

³/₄ cup LIGHT 'N TANGY V8 *or* V8 PICANTE Vegetable Juice

1 tablespoon cornstarch

● Place large plastic bag in deep bowl; add chicken. In 2-cup measure, combine vinaigrette and "V8" juice; pour over chicken. Close bag. *(See tip, page 8.)*

● Refrigerate at least 4 hours or overnight, turning chicken occasionally. Remove chicken from marinade and arrange on rack in broiler pan. Reserve marinade.

● In 1-quart saucepan, stir together cornstarch and reserved marinade until smooth. Over medium heat, cook until sauce boils and thickens, stirring constantly.

● Brush chicken with sauce. Broil 4 inches from heat 15 minutes or until chicken is no longer pink, turning once and brushing often with sauce during cooking.

Serving Suggestion: Tangy Broiled Chicken is served with grapes, cantaloupe, steamed zucchini and rice. Garnish with parsley.

Makes 6 servings.
Prep Time: 5 minutes
Marinating Time: 4 hours or overnight
Cook Time: 20 minutes

CRISPY CHICKEN WITH ASPARAGUS SAUCE

1 egg *or* 2 egg whites

4 skinless, boneless chicken breast halves *or* 8 boneless chicken thighs (about 1 pound)

¹/₂ cup dry bread crumbs

2 tablespoons vegetable oil

1 can (10 ³/₄ ounces) CAMPBELL'S condensed Cream of Asparagus Soup

¹/₃ cup milk

¹/₃ cup water

Grated Parmesan cheese

4 cups prepared long-grain and wild rice mix *or* hot cooked rice

Fresh basil sprigs *and* canned julienne beets for garnish

● In shallow dish, beat egg. Dip chicken into egg. On waxed paper, coat chicken with bread crumbs.

● In 10-inch skillet over medium-low heat, in hot oil, cook chicken 15 minutes or until browned on both sides and no longer pink. Remove; keep warm. Pour off fat.

● In same skillet, combine soup, milk and water. Heat through, stirring occasionally. Spoon soup mixture over chicken. Sprinkle with cheese. Serve with rice. Garnish with basil and beets, if desired.

TIP: Before you begin, start heating water to cook the rice.

Makes 4 servings.
Prep Time: 10 minutes
Cook Time: 20 minutes

ORANGE-GLAZED CHICKEN

1 tablespoon margarine *or* butter

6 skinless, boneless chicken breast halves (about 1 ¹/₂ pounds)

2 tablespoons cornstarch

1 can (14 ¹/₂ ounces) SWANSON Ready To Serve Clear Vegetable Broth

¹/₂ cup sweet orange marmalade *or* apple jelly

1 teaspoon lemon juice

6 cups hot cooked rice

● In 10-inch skillet over medium-high heat, in hot margarine, cook *half* of the chicken 10 minutes or until browned on both sides. Remove; set aside. Repeat with remaining chicken.

● In small bowl, stir together cornstarch, broth, marmalade and lemon juice until smooth. Add to skillet. Cook, uncovered, until mixture boils and thickens, stirring constantly.

● Return chicken to skillet. Reduce heat to low. Cook 5 minutes or until chicken is no longer pink, stirring often. Serve with rice.

TIP: Before you begin, start heating water to cook the rice.

Serving Suggestion: Orange-Glazed Chicken is served with steamed Italian green beans and parslied rice. Garnish with fresh parsley and orange slices.

Makes 6 servings.
Prep Time: 5 minutes
Cook Time: 30 minutes

1 Cook *half* of the chicken 10 minutes or until browned on both sides.

2 In bowl, stir together cornstarch, broth, marmalade and lemon juice until smooth.

3 In same skillet, cook cornstarch mixture until mixture boils and thickens, stirring constantly.

ORANGE-GLAZED CHICKEN

SAVORY CHICKEN AND MUSHROOMS

2 tablespoons margarine *or* butter

4 skinless, boneless chicken breast halves (about 1 pound)

1 ¹/₂ cups fresh broccoli flowerets

1 ¹/₂ cups sliced fresh mushrooms (about 4 ounces)

1 can (10 ³/₄ ounces) CAMPBELL'S condensed Cream of Chicken & Broccoli Soup

¹/₄ cup milk

2 tablespoons Dijon-style mustard

4 cups hot cooked egg noodles (about 4 cups dry)

Cherry tomatoes *and* fresh oregano sprigs for garnish

● In 10-inch skillet over medium-high heat, in *1 tablespoon* hot margarine, cook chicken 15 minutes or until browned on both sides and no longer pink. Remove; keep warm.

● Reduce heat to medium. In same skillet, in remaining *1 tablespoon* hot margarine, cook broccoli and mushrooms until vegetables are tender and liquid is evaporated, stirring often.

● Add soup, milk and mustard. Heat through, stirring occasionally. Spoon soup mixture over chicken. Serve with noodles. Garnish with tomatoes and oregano, if desired.

TIP: When you shop, select chicken that is plump; that's a good indication it will be moist and meaty. Also look for poultry with skin that is clean, white to deep yellow in color and has no bruises or discolorations.

Makes 4 servings.
Prep Time: 15 minutes
Cook Time: 25 minutes

BAKED ONION CHICKEN

1 pouch CAMPBELL'S Dry Onion Soup Mix with Chicken Broth

²/₃ cup dry bread crumbs

¹/₈ teaspoon pepper

1 egg *or* 2 egg whites

2 tablespoons water

12 skinless, boneless chicken thighs *or* 6 skinless, boneless chicken breast halves (about 1 ¹/₂ pounds)

2 tablespoons margarine *or* butter, melted (optional)

● With rolling pin, crush soup mix in pouch. On waxed paper, combine soup mix, bread crumbs and pepper.

● In shallow dish, beat together egg and water. Dip chicken into egg mixture; coat with crumb mixture.

● On baking sheet, arrange chicken. Drizzle with margarine. Bake at 400°F. for 20 minutes or until chicken is no longer pink.

Serving Suggestion: Baked Onion Chicken is served with asparagus and sweet pepper salad. Garnish with lemon and fresh basil.

Makes 6 servings.
Prep Time: 10 minutes
Cook Time: 20 minutes

SPANISH CHICKEN AND MUSHROOMS

SPANISH CHICKEN AND MUSHROOMS

2 tablespoons olive *or* vegetable oil

4 skinless, boneless chicken breast halves (about 1 pound)

2 cups sliced fresh mushrooms (about 6 ounces)

1 can (11 $^1/_8$ ounces) CAMPBELL'S condensed Italian Tomato Soup

$^1/_2$ cup water

$^1/_4$ cup sliced VLASIC *or* EARLY CALIFORNIA Pimento-Stuffed Olives

2 tablespoons Burgundy *or* other dry red wine

4 cups hot cooked egg noodles (about 4 cups dry)

$^1/_4$ cup grated Parmesan cheese (optional)

Fresh oregano sprigs for garnish

● In 10-inch skillet over medium-high heat, in *1 tablespoon* hot oil, cook chicken 10 minutes or until browned on both sides. Remove; set aside.

● Reduce heat to medium. In remaining *1 tablespoon* hot oil, cook mushrooms until tender and liquid is evaporated, stirring often.

● Stir in soup, water, olives and wine. Heat to boiling. Return chicken to skillet. Reduce heat to low. Cover; cook 5 minutes or until chicken is no longer pink, stirring occasionally. Serve with noodles. Sprinkle with cheese. Garnish with oregano, if desired.

TIP: Before you begin, start heating water to cook the noodles.

Makes 4 servings.
Prep Time: 10 minutes
Cook Time: 25 minutes

TIP: The safest way to thaw frozen poultry is to defrost it in the refrigerator. Allow at least 24 hours for every 5 pounds of frozen poultry. Never thaw frozen poultry at room temperature. Try this quick method: Put the package of frozen poultry in a watertight plastic bag and submerge the bag in cold water. Change the water every 30 minutes until poultry is thawed. It will take 30 minutes to 1 hour to thaw 1 pound of frozen poultry.*

*Source: U.S. Department of Agriculture-Food Safety and Inspection Service.

BROCCOLI-CHEESE CHICKEN

1 tablespoon margarine *or* butter

4 skinless, boneless chicken breast halves (about 1 pound)

1 can (10 ³/₄ ounces) CAMPBELL'S condensed Broccoli Cheese Soup

2 cups fresh broccoli flowerets

¹/₃ cup water *or* milk

¹/₈ teaspoon pepper

Cherry tomatoes *and* small patty pan squash for garnish

● In 10-inch skillet over medium-high heat, in hot margarine, cook chicken 10 minutes or until browned on both sides. Remove; set aside.

● In same skillet, combine soup, broccoli, water and pepper. Heat to boiling. Return chicken to skillet. Reduce heat to low. Cover; cook 10 minutes or until chicken is no longer pink and broccoli is tender, stirring often.

● Garnish with tomatoes and squash, if desired.

Asparagus-Cheese Chicken: Prepare Broccoli-Cheese Chicken as directed above, *except* substitute 12 *fresh asparagus spears* (about ³/₄ pound), cut into 2-inch pieces, *or* 1 package (10 ounces) *frozen asparagus cuts*, thawed, for the broccoli.

TIP: Use a sturdy plastic cutting board when cutting raw poultry instead of a wooden board. Since wooden boards are porous, it is difficult to thoroughly wash them.

Makes 4 servings.
Prep Time: 5 minutes
Cook Time: 25 minutes

BROCCOLI-CHEESE CHICKEN

1 Trim tough parts of broccoli stalks. Cut stalks into bite-size pieces called flowerets.

2 In same skillet, combine soup, broccoli, water and pepper.

ℰASY SOUTHWEST CHICKEN

1 tablespoon vegetable oil

4 skinless, boneless chicken breast halves (about 1 pound)

1 can (10 ³/₄ ounces) CAMPBELL'S condensed Golden Corn Soup

1 can (about 8 ounces) stewed tomatoes, cut up

1 teaspoon chili powder

¹/₄ teaspoon garlic powder *or* 2 cloves garlic, minced

¹/₂ cup shredded Monterey Jack cheese (2 ounces)

2 tablespoons finely chopped green pepper

4 cups prepared long-grain and wild rice mix *or* hot cooked rice

Shredded Parmesan cheese, green pepper strips, jalapeño peppers *and* fresh sage leaves for garnish

● In 10-inch skillet over medium-high heat, in hot oil, cook chicken 15 minutes or until browned on both sides and no longer pink. Remove; keep warm. Pour off fat.

● In same skillet, combine soup, tomatoes, chili powder and garlic. Heat to boiling. Reduce heat to low. Cover; cook 5 minutes, stirring occasionally. Spoon soup mixture over chicken. Serve with rice. Sprinkle with cheese. Garnish with green pepper, jalapeño peppers and sage, if desired.

TIP: Chili powder is a ground blend of chili peppers, oregano, cumin, garlic and salt. It has a hot, spicy and sometimes peppery taste and aroma. Some chili powders can include coriander, red pepper (cayenne), cloves, etc. Hot and mild chili powders are available.

Makes 4 servings.
Prep Time: 5 minutes
Cook Time: 20 minutes

Easy CHICKEN PAPRIKASH

1 tablespoon margarine *or* butter

4 skinless, boneless chicken breast halves (about 1 pound)

1 can (10 ³/₄ ounces) CAMPBELL'S condensed Cream of Mushroom Soup

2 teaspoons paprika

¹/₈ teaspoon ground red pepper (cayenne)

4 cups hot cooked egg noodles *or* spaetzle (about 4 cups dry)

¹/₃ cup sour cream *or* plain yogurt

● In 10-inch skillet over medium-high heat, in hot margarine, cook chicken 10 minutes or until browned on both sides. Remove; set aside.

● In same skillet, combine soup, paprika and red pepper. Heat to boiling. Return chicken to skillet. Reduce heat to low. Cover; cook 5 minutes or until chicken is no longer pink, stirring occasionally. Arrange chicken over noodles. Keep warm.

● Stir sour cream into mixture in skillet. Heat through, stirring constantly; spoon over chicken.

Serving Suggestion: Chicken Paprikash is served with hot cooked bow-tie noodles and steamed small zucchini and carrots. Sprinkle chicken with snipped fresh parsley.

Makes 4 servings.
Prep Time: 5 minutes
Cook Time: 25 minutes

LEMON CHICKEN PRIMAVERA

1 tablespoon margarine *or* butter

1 pound skinless, boneless chicken breasts, cut into strips

1 can (10 $1/2$ ounces) FRANCO-AMERICAN Chicken Gravy

1 bag (16 ounces) frozen vegetable combination

3 cloves garlic, minced

2 tablespoons lemon juice

$1/2$ teaspoon dried basil leaves, crushed

$1/8$ teaspoon pepper

4 cups hot cooked spaghetti (about 8 ounces dry)

Fresh basil sprig for garnish

● In 10-inch skillet over medium-high heat, in hot margarine, cook *half* of the chicken until browned, stirring often. Remove; set aside. Repeat with remaining chicken.

● In same skillet, combine gravy, vegetables, garlic, lemon juice, basil and pepper. Heat to boiling. Reduce heat to low. Cover; cook 10 minutes or until vegetables are tender, stirring occasionally. Return chicken to skillet. Heat through, stirring occasionally. Serve over spaghetti. Garnish with basil, if desired.

TIP: To easily remove the skin, lightly crush a garlic clove with the flat side of a wide kitchen knife to crack the skin. The skin will easily slip off. *(See tip, page 6.)*

Makes 4 servings.
Prep Time: 10 minutes
Cook Time: 20 minutes

LEMON CHICKEN PRIMAVERA

ORIENTAL CHICKEN AND NOODLES

2 tablespoons cornstarch

1 can (14 1/2 ounces) SWANSON Ready
To Serve Clear Chicken Broth

1 tablespoon soy sauce

2 packages (3 ounces *each*)
CAMPBELL'S *or* RAMEN PRIDE
Chicken Flavor Ramen Noodle Soup

2 tablespoons vegetable oil

1 pound skinless, boneless chicken
breasts, cut into strips

5 cups cut-up fresh vegetables
(broccoli, green onions, celery
and carrots)

1/4 teaspoon ground ginger

1/8 teaspoon garlic powder *or* 1 clove
garlic, minced

● In small bowl, stir together cornstarch, broth and soy sauce until smooth; set aside. Cook noodles according to package directions. (Reserve seasoning packets for another use.) Drain off most of liquid; set aside.

● In 10-inch skillet or wok over medium-high heat, in *1 tablespoon* hot oil, stir-fry *half* of the chicken until browned. Remove; set aside. Repeat with remaining chicken.

● Reduce heat to medium. In same skillet, in remaining *1 tablespoon* hot oil, stir-fry vegetables, ginger and garlic powder until vegetables are tender-crisp.

● Add reserved cornstarch mixture. Cook until mixture boils and thickens, stirring constantly. Return chicken to skillet. Heat through, stirring occasionally. Serve over noodles. Pass additional *soy sauce*, if desired.

Makes 4 servings.
Prep Time: 20 minutes
Cook Time: 20 minutes

ORIENTAL CHICKEN AND NOODLES

1 Slice chicken into strips.

2 Add noodles to boiling water.

3 Stir noodles during cooking.

$\mathcal{S}$PICY CHICKEN

2 tablespoons margarine *or* butter

1 pound skinless, boneless chicken
  breasts, cut into 1 ¹/₂-inch pieces

1 medium green pepper, chopped
  (about ³/₄ cup)

1 medium onion, cut into thin wedges
  (about ¹/₂ cup)

¹/₂ teaspoon dried oregano leaves,
  crushed

¹/₂ teaspoon paprika

¹/₄ teaspoon pepper

¹/₄ teaspoon ground red pepper
  (cayenne)

1 can (about 16 ounces) stewed
  tomatoes, cut up

1 can (10 ³/₄ ounces) CAMPBELL'S
  condensed Golden Corn Soup

1 cup cooked rice

Fresh rosemary sprigs for garnish

● In 10-inch skillet over medium-high heat, in *1 tablespoon* hot margarine, cook *half* of the chicken until browned, stirring often. Remove; set aside. Repeat with remaining chicken.

● Reduce heat to medium. In same skillet, in remaining *1 tablespoon* hot margarine, cook green pepper, onion, oregano, paprika, pepper and red pepper until vegetables are tender-crisp, stirring often.

● Add tomatoes, soup and rice. Heat to boiling. Return chicken to skillet. Reduce heat to low. Cover; cook 5 minutes or until chicken is no longer pink, stirring occasionally. Garnish with rosemary, if desired.

Makes about 5 ¹/₂ cups or 4 servings.
Prep Time: 20 minutes
Cook Time: 25 minutes

$\mathcal{E}$ASY CHICKEN STROGANOFF

2 tablespoons margarine *or* butter

1 pound skinless, boneless chicken breasts *or* turkey breast cutlets, cut into strips

2 cups sliced fresh mushrooms (about 6 ounces)

1 medium onion, chopped (about 1/2 cup)

1 can (10 3/4 ounces) CAMPBELL'S condensed Cream of Chicken Soup

1/2 cup sour cream *or* plain yogurt

4 cups hot cooked egg noodles (about 4 cups dry)

Snipped fresh parsley *and* very thin strips sweet red and green pepper for garnish

● In 10-inch skillet over medium-high heat, in *1 tablespoon* hot margarine, cook *half* of the chicken until browned, stirring often. Remove; set aside. Repeat with remaining chicken.

● Reduce heat to medium. In same skillet, in remaining *1 tablespoon* hot margarine, cook mushrooms and onion until vegetables are tender and liquid is evaporated, stirring often.

● Stir in soup and sour cream. Heat to boiling. Return chicken to skillet. Heat through, stirring occasionally. Serve over noodles. Sprinkle with parsley. Garnish with red and green pepper, if desired.

TIP: Before you begin, start heating water to cook the noodles.

Makes 4 servings.
Prep Time: 15 minutes
Cook Time: 20 minutes

CHICKEN-MUSHROOM RISOTTO

2 tablespoons margarine *or* butter

³/₄ pound skinless, boneless chicken breasts, cut into 1 ¹/₂-inch pieces

1 cup uncooked regular long-grain rice

1 medium carrot *or* 1 small sweet red pepper, chopped (about ¹/₃ cup)

1 small onion, chopped (about ¹/₄ cup)

1 can (14 ¹/₂ ounces) SWANSON Ready To Serve Clear Chicken Broth

1 can (10 ³/₄ ounces) CAMPBELL'S condensed Cream of Mushroom Soup

¹/₈ teaspoon pepper

¹/₂ cup frozen peas

Fresh rosemary sprigs for garnish

● In 3-quart saucepan over medium-high heat, in *1 tablespoon* hot margarine, cook chicken until browned, stirring often. Remove; set aside.

● Reduce heat to medium. In same saucepan, in remaining *1 tablespoon* hot margarine, cook rice, carrot and onion until rice is browned, stirring constantly. Stir in broth, soup and pepper. Heat to boiling. Reduce heat to low. Cover; cook 15 minutes, stirring occasionally.

● Stir in peas and reserved chicken. Cover; cook 5 minutes or until rice is tender and liquid is absorbed, stirring occasionally. Garnish with rosemary, if desired.

TIP: Consider double-duty chopping! When you have a spare minute chop an extra onion or green pepper. To store, spread the chopped onion or green pepper in a single layer in a shallow baking pan and freeze. Then, break the frozen vegetables into pieces and place in freezer-proof bags. Store in the freezer for up to 1 month. To use, just add the amount you need to the food you are preparing--no need to thaw.

Makes about 4 ¹/₂ cups or 4 servings.
Prep Time: 10 minutes
Cook Time: 35 minutes

CHICKEN-MUSHROOM RISOTTO

1 Cut carrot crosswise into thirds. Cut each third in half lengthwise. With cut side down, cut lengthwise into ¼-inch slices. Stack slices and cut, lengthwise, into thin strips. Gather strips together and cut crosswise to chop.

2 In 3-quart saucepan in hot margarine, cook rice, carrot and onion until rice is browned, stirring constantly.

3 Stir in broth, soup and pepper.

CHICKEN-BROCCOLI DIVAN

1 pound fresh broccoli, cut into flowerets (about 4 cups), cooked and drained *or* 1 package (10 ounces) frozen broccoli spears, cooked and drained

2 cans (5 ounces *each*) SWANSON Premium Chunk White Chicken, drained

1 can (10 3/4 ounces) CAMPBELL'S condensed Cream of Broccoli Soup

1/3 cup milk

1/2 cup shredded Cheddar cheese (2 ounces)

2 tablespoons dry bread crumbs

1 tablespoon margarine *or* butter, melted

● In 9-inch pie plate or 2-quart oblong baking dish, arrange broccoli and chicken. In small bowl, combine soup and milk; pour over broccoli and chicken.

● Sprinkle cheese over soup mixture. In cup, combine bread crumbs and margarine; sprinkle over cheese.

● Bake at 450°F. for 20 minutes or until hot and bubbling.

TIP: Recipe may be doubled and baked in 3-quart oblong baking dish.

TIP: When time is short, micro-cook the fresh broccoli flowerets. In 2-quart microwave-safe casserole, combine broccoli and 2 tablespoons water. Cover with lid. Microwave on HIGH for 6 minutes or until tender-crisp, stirring once during cooking. Drain in colander.

Makes 4 servings.
Prep Time: 15 minutes
Cook Time: 20 minutes

CHICKEN-BROCCOLI DIVAN

CREAMY CHICKEN-BROCCOLI NOODLES

2 packages (3 ounces *each*)
   CAMPBELL'S *or* RAMEN PRIDE
   Chicken Flavor Ramen Noodle Soup

1 can (10 ³/₄ ounces) CAMPBELL'S
   condensed Cream of Mushroom Soup

¹/₂ soup can milk *or* half-and-half

2 tablespoons grated Parmesan cheese
   (optional)

1 ¹/₂ cups cubed cooked chicken

1 ¹/₂ cups cooked broccoli flowerets

6 medium cherry tomatoes, quartered
   (about ¹/₂ cup), optional

Snipped fresh parsley for garnish

● In 2-quart saucepan, prepare noodles according to package directions. Add seasoning packets; drain off most of liquid.

● Stir in mushroom soup, milk and cheese. Add chicken and broccoli. Heat through, stirring occasionally. Stir in tomatoes. Sprinkle with parsley, if desired.

TIP: You may substitute 2 cans (5 ounces *each*) SWANSON Premium Chunk White Chicken, drained, for the cooked chicken.

Makes about 6 1/2 cups or 4 servings.
Prep Time: 10 minutes
Cook Time: 10 minutes

$\mathcal{H}$OMESTYLE CHICKEN AND BISCUITS

1 can (10 ¹/₂ ounces)
FRANCO-AMERICAN Chicken Gravy

¹/₂ teaspoon poultry seasoning

2 cans (5 ounces *each*) SWANSON
Premium Chunk White Chicken,
drained

1 package (10 ounces) frozen mixed
vegetables

1 package (4 ¹/₂ ounces) refrigerated
biscuits (6)

● In 1¹/₂-quart casserole, combine gravy and poultry seasoning; stir in chicken and frozen vegetables.

● Bake at 400°F. for 15 minutes or until mixture begins to bubble. Meanwhile, cut each biscuit in half.

● Remove casserole from oven; stir. Arrange biscuit halves on chicken mixture around edge and in center of casserole. Bake 15 minutes more or until biscuits are golden.

Makes about 3 cups or 4 servings.
Prep Time: 5 minutes
Cook Time: 30 minutes

EASY CHICKEN ENCHILADAS

2 cans (5 ounces *each*) SWANSON
Premium Chunk White Chicken,
drained

1 ¹/₂ cups shredded Cheddar cheese
(6 ounces)

1 can (4 ounces) chopped green chilies,
drained (optional)

1 small onion, chopped (about ¹/₄ cup)

1 can (10 ounces) enchilada sauce

8 corn tortillas (6 inches *each*)

Shredded lettuce (optional)

Sour cream (optional)

Diced tomatoes (optional)

● In medium bowl, combine chicken, *1 cup* cheese, chilies and onion.

● In bottom of 3-quart oblong baking dish, spread ¹/₂ *can* enchilada sauce; set aside.

● To assemble enchiladas: Along one side of each tortilla, spread about ¹/₃ *cup* chicken mixture. Roll up each tortilla, jelly-roll fashion. Place seam-side down in sauce in baking dish.

● Pour remaining ¹/₂ *can* enchilada sauce over enchiladas. Sprinkle with remaining ¹/₂ *cup* cheese. Cover; bake at 350°F. for 25 minutes or until hot. Top with lettuce, sour cream and tomatoes.

Makes 4 servings.
Prep Time: 20 minutes
Cook Time: 25 minutes

❶ In bowl, combine chicken, *1 cup* cheese, chilies and onion.

EASY CHICKEN ENCHILADAS

2 In bottom of baking dish, spread *¹/₂ can* enchilada sauce.

3 Roll up each tortilla. Place in baking dish, seam-side down.

4 Pour remaining enchilada sauce over filled tortillas. Sprinkle with remaining cheese.

CHICKEN AND VEGETABLE STIR-FRY

2 tablespoons cornstarch

1 can (14 ¹/₂ ounces) SWANSON Ready
   To Serve Clear Chicken Broth

1 tablespoon soy sauce

¹/₂ teaspoon ground ginger *or*
   1 teaspoon grated fresh ginger

1 tablespoon vegetable oil

2 medium carrots, cut into matchstick-
   thin strips (about 1 cup)

1 small zucchini, diagonally sliced
   (about 1 cup) *or* 1 cup fresh broccoli
   flowerets

¹/₂ cup quartered fresh mushrooms

2 cans (5 ounces *each*) SWANSON
   Premium Chunk White Chicken,
   drained

4 cups hot cooked rice

1 medium green onion, diagonally
   sliced (about 2 tablespoons), optional

● In small bowl, stir together cornstarch, chicken broth, soy sauce and ginger until smooth; set aside.

● In 10-inch skillet or wok over medium heat, in hot oil, stir-fry carrots, zucchini and mushrooms until tender-crisp.

● Stir in reserved cornstarch mixture. Cook until mixture boils and thickens, stirring constantly.

● Gently stir in chicken; heat through, stirring occasionally. Serve over rice. Sprinkle with onion.

Makes about 3 ¹/₂ cups or 4 servings.
Prep Time: 15 minutes
Cook Time: 10 minutes

COUNTRY CHICKEN SOUP

3 cans (14 $^{1}/_{2}$ ounces *each*) SWANSON Ready To Serve Clear Chicken Broth

$^{1}/_{2}$ cup uncooked regular long-grain rice

1 medium carrot, sliced (about $^{1}/_{2}$ cup)

1 rib celery, sliced (about $^{1}/_{2}$ cup)

1 small onion, finely chopped (about $^{1}/_{4}$ cup)

$^{1}/_{2}$ teaspoon snipped fresh thyme leaves *or* $^{1}/_{8}$ teaspoon dried thyme leaves, crushed

$^{1}/_{8}$ teaspoon poultry seasoning

2 cans (5 ounces *each*) SWANSON Premium Chunk White Chicken, undrained

● In 3-quart saucepan, combine broth, rice, carrot, celery, onion, thyme and poultry seasoning. Over medium heat, heat to boiling. Reduce heat to low. Cover; cook 20 minutes or until vegetables and rice are tender, stirring occasionally.

● Add *undrained* chicken; heat through, stirring occasionally.

Makes about 6 $^{1}/_{2}$ cups or 4 servings.
Prep Time: 10 minutes
Cook Time: 25 minutes

HERBED TURKEY AND MUSHROOMS

2 tablespoons margarine *or* butter

4 turkey breast tenderloin steaks *or* turkey breast slices (about 1 pound)

1 cup sliced fresh mushrooms (about 3 ounces)

$1/4$ teaspoon dried rosemary leaves, crushed

1 can (10 $1/2$ ounces) FRANCO-AMERICAN Turkey Gravy

1 teaspoon lemon juice

1 tablespoon snipped fresh parsley *or* 1 teaspoon dried parsley flakes

1 tablespoon sour cream

● In 10-inch skillet over medium-high heat, in *1 tablespoon* hot margarine, cook *half* of the turkey 3 minutes or until browned on both sides. Remove; set aside. Repeat with remaining turkey.

● Reduce heat to medium. In same skillet, in remaining *1 tablespoon* hot margarine, cook mushrooms and rosemary until mushrooms are tender and liquid is evaporated, stirring often.

● Stir in gravy and lemon juice. Heat to boiling. Return turkey to skillet. Reduce heat to low. Cover; cook 5 minutes or until turkey is no longer pink, stirring gravy mixture occasionally. Remove turkey; keep warm. Stir parsley and sour cream into gravy mixture; spoon over turkey.

TIP: Turkey breast tenderloin steaks are cut *lengthwise* from the breast. They are long, thin cuts that resemble fish fillets. Use them as you would skinless, boneless chicken breast halves; cooking times may vary. Turkey breast slices and cutlets are cut *crosswise* from the breast.

Serving Suggestion: Herbed Turkey and Mushrooms is served with steamed snow peas, small potatoes and baby carrots. Garnish with fresh rosemary.

Makes 4 servings.
Prep Time: 5 minutes
Cook Time: 15 minutes

HERBED TURKEY AND MUSHROOMS

ORANGE-GLAZED TURKEY

4 ½- to 5-pound turkey breast

Salt

Pepper

2 cans (10 1/2 ounces *each*)
   FRANCO-AMERICAN Turkey Gravy

²/₃ cup sweet orange marmalade

1 tablespoon Dijon-style mustard

Orange slices *and* fresh rosemary
   sprigs for garnish

● Rinse turkey with cold running water; drain well. On rack in shallow roasting pan, place turkey breast-side up. Season with salt and pepper. Insert oven-safe meat thermometer into thickest part of breast, *not touching bone*. Roast at 325°F. for 2 hours.

● Meanwhile, to make glaze: In 1½-quart saucepan, combine gravy, marmalade and mustard. Over medium heat, heat to boiling, stirring constantly; set aside. During last 30 minutes of roasting, brush turkey with ½ *cup* glaze.

● Use ½ *cup* glaze to baste turkey; set remaining glaze aside. Roast turkey 30 minutes more, or until internal temperature reaches 180°F. to 185°F and juices run clear.

● Transfer turkey to platter, reserving pan drippings. Let turkey stand, covered, 10 minutes for easier carving. Skim fat from drippings. Stir remaining glaze into drippings in roasting pan. Over medium heat, heat through, stirring to loosen browned bits. Garnish with orange slices and rosemary, if desired.

TIP: To get an accurate reading when using a meat thermometer, insert the thermometer into the thickest part of the turkey breast. Make sure the tip of the thermometer *does not touch* any bone or fat or the bottom of the pan. When the meat reaches 180°F. to 185°F., push the thermometer into the turkey breast a little farther. If the temperature drops, continue cooking. If the temperature remains the same, the turkey breast is done.

Makes 6 servings.
Prep Time: 5 minutes
Cook Time: 2 ½ hours
Stand Time: 10 minutes

ORANGE-GLAZED TURKEY

1 Place turkey breast-side up, on rack in roasting pan. Insert meat thermometer into thickest part of breast, *not touching bone.*

2 During last 30 minutes of roasting, brush turkey with *1/2 cup* glaze.

3 Cut turkey, across the grain, into thin slices.

*I*TALIANO TURKEY AND PASTA

3 teaspoons olive oil

1 pound turkey breast cutlets *or* slices,
cut into strips

1 can (26 ¹/₂ ounces) CAMPBELL'S
Homestyle Spaghetti Sauce

1 medium onion, cut into thin wedges
(about ¹/₂ cup)

2 tablespoons grated Parmesan cheese

¹/₂ teaspoon dried rosemary leaves,
crushed

¹/₈ teaspoon crushed red pepper

6 cups hot cooked corkscrew macaroni
(about 5 cups dry)

Shredded Parmesan cheese *and* fresh
oregano sprigs for garnish

● In 10-inch skillet over medium-high heat, in
1 ¹/₂ teaspoons hot oil, cook *half* of the turkey
until browned, stirring often. Remove; set
aside. Repeat with remaining oil and turkey.
Pour off fat.

● In same skillet, combine spaghetti sauce,
onion, 2 tablespoons cheese, rosemary and
red pepper. Heat to boiling. Reduce heat to
low. Cover; cook 5 minutes or until onion is
tender, stirring occasionally.

● Return turkey to skillet. Heat through, stirring occasionally. Serve over macaroni.
Garnish with *shredded Parmesan cheese* and
oregano, if desired.

Makes 6 servings.
Prep Time: 15 minutes
Cook Time: 20 minutes

TURKEY AND STUFFING BAKE

1 package (7 ounces) PEPPERIDGE
FARM Cubed Herb Seasoned Stuffing

1 cup whole berry cranberry sauce

1/2 cup chopped walnuts *or* pecans

2 cans (5 ounces *each*) SWANSON
Premium Chunk White Turkey,
drained

1 can (10 1/2 ounces)
FRANCO-AMERICAN Turkey Gravy

● Prepare stuffing according to package directions.

● In medium bowl, combine prepared stuffing, cranberry sauce and nuts; set aside.

● In 2-quart oblong baking dish, arrange turkey. Pour gravy over turkey. Spoon stuffing mixture in even layer over all.

● Bake at 400°F. for 15 minutes or until hot and bubbling.

Makes 4 servings.
Prep Time: 15 minutes
Cook Time: 15 minutes

GARDEN TURKEY AND STUFFING

1/4 cup margarine *or* butter

3 medium carrots, chopped
(about 1 cup)

2 ribs celery, chopped (about 1 cup)

1 large onion, chopped (about 1 cup)

1/4 cup all-purpose flour

1 can (10 1/2 ounces) CAMPBELL'S
condensed Chicken Broth

1 cup milk

1 package (7 ounces) PEPPERIDGE
FARM Cubed Herb Seasoned Stuffing

2 cans (5 ounces *each*) SWANSON
Premium Chunk White Turkey *or*
Chicken, drained

1 cup shredded Cheddar cheese
(4 ounces)

● In 3-quart saucepan over medium heat, in hot margarine, cook carrots, celery and onion until tender. Add flour; cook 1 minute, stirring constantly. Gradually add broth and milk, stirring constantly. Cook until mixture boils and thickens, stirring constantly.

● Add stuffing and turkey; toss to coat. Spoon into 2-quart oblong baking dish. Bake at 350°F. for 35 minutes. Sprinkle with cheese. Bake 5 minutes more or until the cheese is melted.

Makes 6 servings.
Prep Time: 15 minutes
Cook Time: 50 minutes

PEPPER STEAK

1 pound boneless beef sirloin *or* top round steak, 3/4 inch thick

2 tablespoons vegetable oil

2 cups sweet pepper strips (green, red *and/or* yellow)

1 medium onion, cut into wedges

1/4 teaspoon garlic powder *or* 2 cloves garlic, minced

1 can (10 3/4 ounces) CAMPBELL'S condensed Beefy Mushroom Soup

1 tablespoon soy sauce

1/2 teaspoon ground ginger

4 cups hot cooked rice

● Slice beef across the grain into thin strips.

● In 10-inch skillet or wok over medium-high heat, in *1 tablespoon* hot oil, stir-fry *half* of the beef until browned. Remove; set aside. Repeat with remaining beef.

● Reduce heat to medium. In same skillet in remaining *1 tablespoon* hot oil, stir-fry peppers, onion and garlic until vegetables are tender-crisp.

● Stir in soup, soy sauce and ginger. Heat to boiling. Return beef to skillet. Heat through, stirring occasionally. Serve over rice.

TIP: To make slicing beef easier, freeze beef 1 hour.

TIP: Prepare Pepper Steak as directed above, *except* substitute 1 tablespoon *oyster sauce* for the soy sauce and 1 teaspoon grated *fresh ginger* for the ground ginger.

Makes about 4 cups mixture or 4 servings.
Prep Time: 15 minutes
Cook Time: 20 minutes

PEPPER STEAK

SIMPLE SALISBURY STEAK

1 can (10 ³/₄ ounces) CAMPBELL'S condensed Cream of Mushroom Soup

1 pound ground beef

¹/₃ cup dry bread crumbs

1 small onion, finely chopped (about ¹/₄ cup)

1 egg, beaten

1 tablespoon vegetable oil

1 ¹/₂ cups sliced fresh mushrooms (about 4 ounces)

● In large bowl, mix thoroughly ¹/₄ *cup* soup, beef, bread crumbs, onion and egg. Shape firmly into 6 oval patties of even thickness.

● In 10-inch skillet over medium-high heat, in hot oil, cook *half* of the patties until browned on both sides. Remove; set aside. Repeat with remaining patties. Pour off fat.

● In same skillet, combine remaining soup and mushrooms. Heat to boiling. Return patties to skillet. Reduce heat to low. Cover; cook 20 minutes or until patties are no longer pink, turning patties occasionally.

Serving Suggestion: Simple Salisbury Steak is served with steamed Brussels sprouts and carrots and fried potatoes. Garnish with parsley.

Makes 6 servings.
Prep Time: 10 minutes
Cook Time: 30 minutes

BURGUNDY BEEF

1 pound boneless beef sirloin steak, ³/4 inch thick

1 tablespoon margarine *or* butter

1 bag (16 ounces) frozen vegetable combination (zucchini, cauliflower and carrots)

1 can (10 ¹/4 ounces) FRANCO-AMERICAN Beef Gravy

¹/4 cup tomato paste

¹/4 cup Burgundy *or* other dry red wine

¹/8 teaspoon garlic powder *or* 1 clove garlic, minced

4 cups hot cooked rice

Fresh parsley sprigs for garnish

● Cut beef into 1-inch pieces.

● In 10-inch skillet over medium-high heat, in hot margarine, cook *half* of the beef until browned, stirring often. Remove; set aside. Repeat with remaining beef.

● In same skillet, combine vegetables, gravy, tomato paste, wine and garlic. Heat to boiling. Return beef to skillet. Reduce heat to low. Cover; cook 10 minutes or until vegetables are tender, stirring occasionally. Serve over rice. Garnish with parsley, if desired.

Makes about 4 cups or 4 servings.
Prep Time: 10 minutes
Cook Time: 25 minutes

BURGUNDY BEEF

BROCCOLI-BEEF STIR-FRY

1 pound boneless beef sirloin *or* top round steak, 3/4 inch thick

2 tablespoons vegetable oil

2 cups fresh broccoli flowerets

1/2 teaspoon ground ginger

1/4 teaspoon garlic powder *or* 2 cloves garlic, minced

1 can (10 3/4 ounces) CAMPBELL'S condensed Tomato Soup

2 tablespoons soy sauce

1 tablespoon vinegar

4 cups hot cooked rice

Fresh parsley sprigs *and* very thin strips lemon peel for garnish

● Slice beef across the grain into thin strips.

● In wok or 10-inch skillet over medium-high heat, in *1 tablespoon* hot oil, stir-fry *half* of the beef until browned. Remove; set aside. Repeat with remaining beef.

● Reduce heat to medium. In same skillet, in remaining *1 tablespoon* hot oil, stir-fry broccoli, ginger and garlic powder until broccoli is tender-crisp.

● Stir in soup, soy sauce and vinegar. Heat to boiling. Return beef to skillet. Heat through, stirring occasionally. Serve over rice. Garnish with parsley and lemon peel, if desired.

TIP: To make slicing easier, freeze the beef 1 hour.

Makes about 3 cups or 4 servings.
Prep Time: 15 minutes
Cook Time: 20 minutes

BROCCOLI-BEEF STIR-FRY

1 Slice beef across the grain into thin strips.

2 Return beef to wok.

LONDON BROIL WITH MUSHROOM SAUCE

1 ½ pounds beef top round steak, about 1 ½ inches thick

2 tablespoons margarine *or* butter

2 cups sliced fresh mushrooms (about 6 ounces)

1 medium onion, chopped (about ½ cup)

1 can (10 ¾ ounces) CAMPBELL'S condensed Cream of Mushroom Soup

¼ cup water

2 teaspoons Worcestershire sauce

Celery leaves, cherry tomatoes *and* fresh herbs for garnish

● On unheated rack in broiler pan, arrange steak. Broil 4 inches from heat until desired doneness, turning once during cooking. (Allow about 25 minutes for medium, 160°F.)

● Meanwhile, in 10-inch skillet over medium heat, in hot margarine, cook mushrooms and onion until vegetables are tender and liquid is evaporated, stirring often. Add soup, water and Worcestershire sauce. Heat through, stirring occasionally.

● Thinly slice meat diagonally across the grain. Serve with sauce.

● Garnish with celery leaves, tomatoes and herbs, if desired.

Makes about 1 ½ cups sauce or 6 servings.
Prep Time: 10 minutes
Cook Time: 25 minutes

QUICK BEEF STROGANOFF

1 pound boneless beef sirloin *or* top round steak, ³/₄ inch thick

2 tablespoons margarine *or* butter

1 large onion, cut into thin wedges (about 1 cup)

1 can (10 ¹/₂ ounces) FRANCO-AMERICAN Mushroom Gravy

1 cup sliced fresh mushrooms (about 3 ounces)

¹/₂ teaspoon paprika

¹/₂ cup sour cream

4 cups hot cooked egg noodles (about 4 cups dry)

Fresh parsley for garnish

● Slice beef across the grain into thin strips.

● In 10-inch skillet over medium-high heat, in *1 tablespoon* hot margarine, cook *half* of the beef and onion until beef is browned and onion is tender, stirring often. Remove; set aside. Repeat with remaining margarine, beef and onion.

● In same skillet, combine gravy, mushrooms and *¹/₂ teaspoon* paprika. Heat to boiling. Return beef and onion to skillet. Reduce heat to low. Heat through, stirring occasionally. Stir in sour cream. Serve over noodles. Sprinkle with snipped parsley and additional *paprika*. Garnish with parsley, if desired.

TIP: To make slicing easier, freeze beef 1 hour.

Makes about 3 ¹/₂ cups or 4 servings.
Prep Time: 10 minutes
Cook Time: 15 minutes

$\mathcal{T}$WO-BEAN CHILI

1 pound ground beef

1 large green pepper, chopped (about 1 cup)

1 large onion, chopped (about 1 cup)

2 tablespoons chili powder

1/4 teaspoon pepper

3 cups CAMPBELL'S Tomato Juice

1 can (about 15 ounces) kidney beans, rinsed and drained

1 can (about 15 ounces) great northern beans, rinsed and drained

Sliced green onions, shredded Cheddar cheese *and* sour cream for garnish

● In 6-quart Dutch oven over medium-high heat, cook beef, green pepper, onion, chili powder and pepper until beef is browned and vegetables are tender, stirring to separate meat. Spoon off fat.

● Add tomato juice, kidney beans and great northern beans. Heat to boiling. Reduce heat to low. Cover; cook 20 minutes to blend flavors, stirring occasionally.

● Sprinkle with green onions and cheese. Top with sour cream, if desired.

Makes about 6 cups or 6 servings.
Prep Time: 10 minutes
Cook Time: 35 minutes

$\mathcal{B}$EEFED-UP CHILI

1 1/2 pounds ground beef

1 large onion, chopped (about 1 cup)

1 can (10 1/4 ounces) FRANCO-AMERICAN Beef Gravy

1 can (about 15 ounces) kidney beans, undrained

2 tablespoons chili powder

2 tablespoons ketchup

1/8 teaspoon garlic powder *or* 1 clove garlic, minced

1 large jalapeño pepper, seeded and finely chopped (optional)

5 cups hot cooked rice

Shredded Cheddar cheese *and* fresh parsley sprigs for garnish

● In 10-inch skillet over medium-high heat, cook beef and onion until beef is browned and onion is tender, stirring to separate meat. Spoon off fat.

● Add gravy, *undrained* beans, chili powder, ketchup, garlic powder and jalapeño pepper. Heat to boiling. Reduce heat to low. Cook 15 minutes to blend flavors, stirring occasionally. Serve over rice. Sprinkle with cheese. Garnish with parsley, if desired.

Makes about 5 1/2 cups or 5 servings.
Prep Time: 10 minutes
Cook Time: 25 minutes

TWO-BEAN CHILI (TOP)
BEEFED-UP CHILI (BOTTOM)

SKILLET BEEF 'N' NOODLES

2 packages (3 ounces *each*) CAMPBELL'S *or* RAMEN PRIDE Beef Flavor Ramen Noodle Soup

1 pound ground beef

1 medium onion, chopped (about $^1/_2$ cup)

1 can (11 $^1/_8$ ounces) CAMPBELL'S condensed Italian Tomato Soup

$^1/_2$ soup can water

1 teaspoon prepared mustard

1 teaspoon Worcestershire sauce

Generous dash pepper

Grated Parmesan cheese

Fresh basil leaves for garnish

● Prepare noodles according to package directions. Add seasoning packets; drain off most of liquid. Set aside.

● Meanwhile, in 10-inch skillet over medium-high heat, cook beef and onion until beef is browned and onion is tender, stirring to separate meat. Spoon off fat.

● Stir in tomato soup, water, mustard, Worcestershire sauce and pepper. Reduce heat to low. Add reserved noodles. Heat through, stirring occasionally. Sprinkle with cheese. Garnish with basil, if desired.

TIP: Before serving, stir in $^1/_2$ cup *sour cream*. Sprinkle with snipped *fresh parsley*.

Makes about 5 $^1/_2$ cups or 4 servings.
Prep Time: 5 minutes
Cook Time: 15 minutes

QUICK AND EASY STIR-FRY

1 pound boneless beef sirloin *or* top round steak, 3/4 inch thick

2 tablespoons vegetable oil

2 cups fresh broccoli flowerets

1 1/2 cups sliced fresh mushrooms (about 4 ounces)

2 large green onions, cut diagonally into 2-inch pieces (about 1/2 cup)

1 can (10 1/2 ounces) FRANCO-AMERICAN Mushroom Gravy

1 tablespoon soy sauce

4 cups hot cooked rice

● Slice beef across the grain into thin strips.

● In 10-inch skillet or wok over medium-high heat, in *1 tablespoon* hot oil, stir-fry *half* of the beef until browned. Remove; set aside. Repeat with remaining beef.

● Reduce heat to medium. In same skillet, in remaining *1 tablespoon* hot oil, stir-fry broccoli, mushrooms and green onions until vegetables are tender-crisp.

● Stir in gravy and soy sauce. Heat to boiling. Return beef to skillet. Reduce heat to low. Heat through, stirring occasionally. Serve over rice. Pass additional *soy sauce,* if desired.

TIP: To make slicing easier, freeze beef 1 hour.

Makes 4 servings.
Prep Time: 15 minutes
Cook Time: 20 minutes

SAVORY PORK AND VEGETABLES

2 tablespoons margarine *or* butter

4 boneless pork chops, each ³/₄ inch thick (about 1 pound)

1 ¹/₂ cups sliced fresh mushrooms (about 4 ounces)

¹/₂ teaspoon dried rosemary leaves, crushed

1 can (10 ³/₄ ounces) CAMPBELL'S condensed Cream of Mushroom Soup

¹/₂ pound fresh green beans, cut into 2-inch pieces (about 1 ¹/₂ cups) *or* 1 package (9 ounces) frozen green beans

2 tablespoons water

4 cups hot cooked egg noodles (about 4 cups dry)

● In 10-inch skillet over medium-high heat, in *1 tablespoon* hot margarine, cook chops 10 minutes or until browned on both sides. Remove; set aside.

● Reduce heat to medium. In same skillet, in remaining *1 tablespoon* hot margarine, cook mushrooms and rosemary until mushrooms are tender and liquid is evaporated, stirring often.

● Stir in soup, beans and water. Heat to boiling. Return chops to skillet. Reduce heat to low. Cover; cook 10 minutes or until chops are no longer pink and green beans are tender, stirring occasionally. Serve with noodles.

TIP: You may substitute ¹/₂ pound fresh sugar snap peas (about 1 ¹/₂ cups), *or* 1 package (10 ounces) frozen sugar snap peas for the green beans.

Serving Suggestion: Savory Pork and Vegetables is served with hot cooked noodles and steamed asparagus. Garnish with cherry tomato and small kale leaves.

Makes 4 servings.
Prep Time: 10 minutes
Cook Time: 30 minutes

SAVORY PORK AND VEGETABLES

PORK FAJITAS

1 ¹/₂ pounds pork tenderloin

1 cup refrigerated MARIE'S ZESTY Fat Free Classic Herb Vinaigrette

¹/₄ cup soy sauce

1 medium onion, chopped (about ¹/₂ cup)

¹/₂ cup coarsely chopped tomato

8 flour tortillas (8 inches *each*)

¹/₂ cup shredded Cheddar cheese (2 ounces)

2 cups shredded lettuce

● Place large plastic bag in deep bowl; add pork. In 2-cup measure, combine ¹/₂ *cup* vinaigrette and soy sauce; pour over pork. Close bag. (*See tip, page 8.*)

● Refrigerate at least 4 hours or overnight, turning pork occasionally. Remove pork from marinade and arrange on rack in broiler pan. Discard marinade. Broil 4 inches from heat 20 minutes or until pork is no longer pink, turning once during cooking (160°F. for medium, 170°F. for well done).

● In medium bowl, combine remaining ¹/₂ *cup* vinaigrette, onion and tomato; set aside.

● Heat tortillas according to package directions. Thinly slice pork. Arrange ¹/₂ cup pork down center of *each* tortilla. Top *each* with 2 tablespoons vinaigrette mixture, 1 tablespoon cheese and ¹/₄ cup lettuce. Roll or fold tortilla around filling. Serve, as shown, with assorted *crisp vegetables*, if desired.

Chicken Fajitas: Prepare Pork Fajitas as directed above, *except* substitute 6 *skinless, boneless chicken breast halves* for the pork. Reduce broiling time to 15 minutes total.

Makes 8 servings.
Prep Time: 10 minutes
Marinating Time: 4 hours or overnight
Cook Time: 20 minutes

PORK FAJITAS

1 Remove several leaves from lettuce. Stack leaves and slice into thin strips.

2 Arrange *1/2 cup* sliced cooked pork down center of *each* tortilla. Top with vinaigrette mixture, cheese and lettuce.

3 Roll or fold tortilla around filling.

SAUSAGE AND PEPPERS

1 tablespoon olive oil

1 pound sweet Italian pork sausage, cut into 1-inch pieces

2 medium green peppers, cut into strips (about 2 cups)

1 medium onion, sliced and separated into rings (about $^1/_2$ cup)

1 teaspoon dried oregano leaves, crushed

$^1/_8$ teaspoon garlic powder *or* 1 clove garlic, minced

1 can (10 $^1/_4$ ounces) FRANCO-AMERICAN Beef Gravy

$^1/_4$ cup grated Parmesan cheese

4 cups hot cooked spaghetti (about 8 ounces dry)

● In 10-inch skillet over medium-high heat, in hot oil, cook sausage, green peppers, onion, oregano and garlic powder until sausage is no longer pink and vegetables are tender, stirring often.

● Add gravy and cheese. Reduce heat to low. Heat through, stirring occasionally. Serve over spaghetti. Sprinkle with additional grated *Parmesan cheese.*

Makes 4 servings.
Prep Time: 10 minutes
Cook Time: 15 minutes

PORK CHOPS ITALIANO

1 tablespoon vegetable oil

6 pork chops, each $^1/_2$ inch thick (about 1 $^1/_2$ pounds)

2 cups PREGO EXTRA CHUNKY Mushroom & Green Pepper Spaghetti Sauce

6 cups hot cooked rice

● In 10-inch skillet over medium-high heat, in hot oil, cook *half* of the chops 5 minutes or until browned on both sides. Remove; set aside. Repeat with remaining chops. Pour off fat.

● In same skillet, heat spaghetti sauce to boiling. Return chops to skillet. Reduce heat to low. Cover; cook 5 minutes or until chops are no longer pink, stirring occasionally. Serve with rice.

Makes 6 servings.
Prep Time: 5 minutes
Cook Time: 20 minutes

PORK AND CORN STUFFING BAKE

1 can (10 $^3/_4$ ounces) CAMPBELL'S condensed Golden Corn Soup

1 $^1/_2$ cups PEPPERIDGE FARM Corn Bread Stuffing

1 small onion, chopped (about $^1/_4$ cup)

$^1/_4$ cup chopped celery

$^1/_2$ teaspoon paprika

4 boneless pork chops, each $^3/_4$ inch thick (about 1 pound)

1 tablespoon packed brown sugar

1 teaspoon spicy brown mustard

● In bowl, combine soup, stuffing, onion, celery and paprika. In 9-inch greased pie plate, spoon stuffing mixture. Arrange chops on stuffing, pressing lightly into stuffing.

● In cup, combine sugar and mustard. Spread mixture evenly over chops.

● Bake at 400°F. for 30 minutes or until chops are no longer pink. Transfer chops to serving platter. Stir stuffing; serve with chops.

Fruited Pork Stuffing Bake: Prepare Pork and Corn Stuffing Bake as directed above, *except* add $^1/_3$ cup *raisins or chopped, mixed dried fruit* with the stuffing.

Serving Suggestion: Pork and Corn Stuffing Bake is served with steamed carrots and small sunburst squash. Garnish with fresh parsley.

Makes 4 servings.
Prep Time: 10 minutes
Cook Time: 30 minutes

GLAZED PORK CHOPS

1 tablespoon margarine *or* butter

6 pork chops, each ³/₄ inch thick
(about 2 pounds)

1 cup water

1 pouch CAMPBELL'S Dry Onion Soup
and Recipe Mix

2 tablespoons packed brown sugar

1 medium apple, cored and sliced

2 teaspoons cornstarch

● In 10-inch skillet over medium-high heat, in hot margarine, cook *half* of chops 10 minutes or until browned on both sides. Remove; set aside. Repeat with remaining chops.

● In same skillet, combine ³/₄ *cup* water, onion soup mix and sugar. Add sliced apple, stirring to coat with sauce. Heat to boiling. Return chops to skillet. Reduce heat to low. Cover; cook 10 minutes or until chops are no longer pink, stirring occasionally.

● Meanwhile, in cup, stir together cornstarch and remaining ¹/₄ *cup* water until smooth.

● Remove chops and apples to platter; keep warm. Over medium heat, heat sauce mixture to boiling. Add cornstarch mixture. Cook until mixture boils and thickens, stirring constantly. Spoon over pork and apples.

Serving Suggestion: Glazed Pork Chops are served with steamed zucchini and potatoes. Garnish with fresh rosemary and oregano.

Makes 6 servings.
Prep Time: 5 minutes
Cook Time: 40 minutes

QUICK CASSOULET

1 can (10 ³/₄ ounces) CAMPBELL'S condensed Creamy Onion Soup

1 can (10 ³/₄ ounces) CAMPBELL'S condensed Tomato Soup

1 cup water

1 can (about 16 ounces) small white beans, rinsed and drained

³/₄ pound kielbasa, cut into ¹/₂-inch slices

4 small potatoes (about ³/₄ pound), peeled and quartered

3 medium carrots, cut into ¹/₂-inch pieces (about 1 cup)

1 ¹/₂ teaspoons snipped fresh thyme leaves *or* ¹/₂ teaspoon dried thyme leaves, crushed

¹/₈ teaspoon pepper

1 bay leaf

Fresh thyme *or* parsley sprig for garnish

● In 4-quart saucepan, combine soups and water. Add beans, kielbasa, potatoes, carrots, thyme, pepper and bay leaf. Over medium heat, heat to boiling, stirring occasionally.

● Reduce heat to low. Cover; cook 25 minutes or until vegetables are tender, stirring occasionally. Discard bay leaf. Garnish with thyme, if desired.

TIP: Prepare Quick Cassoulet as directed above, *except* reduce water to ³/₄ cup and add ¹/₄ cup *Chablis or other dry white wine.*

Makes about 8 cups or 5 servings.
Prep Time: 10 minutes
Cook Time: 35 minutes

QUICK CASSOULET

$\mathcal{P}$ORK MOZZARELLA

1 pouch CAMPBELL'S Dry Onion Soup Mix with Chicken Broth

1/3 cup dry bread crumbs

1/8 teaspoon pepper

1 egg *or* 2 egg whites

2 tablespoons water

6 boneless pork chops, each 3/4 inch thick (about 1 1/2 pounds)

1 1/2 cups CAMPBELL'S Traditional Spaghetti Sauce

1 cup shredded mozzarella cheese (4 ounces)

● With rolling pin, crush soup mix in pouch. On waxed paper, combine soup mix, bread crumbs and pepper.

● In shallow dish, beat together egg and water. Dip chops into egg mixture; coat with soup mixture.

● In 2-quart oblong baking dish, arrange chops. Bake at 400°F. for 20 minutes.

● Pour spaghetti sauce over chops. Sprinkle with cheese. Bake 5 minutes more or until chops are no longer pink and sauce is hot and bubbling.

TIP: You may substitute 6 bone-in pork chops, each cut 3/4 inch thick (about 2 pounds), for the boneless chops. Use 3-quart oblong baking dish. Bake 30 minutes before topping with spaghetti sauce. Continue as directed.

Serving Suggestion: Pork Mozzarella is served with steamed zucchini and carrots and hot cooked linguine. Garnish with fresh oregano.

Makes 6 servings.
Prep Time: 10 minutes
Cook Time: 25 minutes

PORK MOZZARELLA

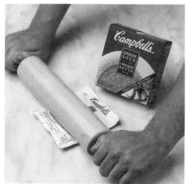

1 With rolling pin, crush soup mixture in pouch.

2 Dip chops into egg mixture; coat each with soup mixture. Arrange chops in baking dish.

3 Pour spaghetti sauce over partially-baked chops. Sprinkle with cheese.

$\mathscr{S}$WEET 'N' SAUCY CHOPS

1 tablespoon vegetable oil

6 pork chops, each ³/₄ inch thick
(about 2 pounds)

1 ¹/₂ cups CAMPBELL'S Tomato Juice

1 small onion, sliced and separated into
rings (about ¹/₄ cup)

1 tablespoon packed brown sugar

1 tablespoon soy sauce

¹/₈ teaspoon ground ginger

¹/₈ teaspoon garlic powder *or* 1 clove
garlic, minced

1 tablespoon cornstarch

6 cups hot cooked mostaccioli *or* other
pasta (about 6 cups dry)

● In 10-inch skillet over medium-high heat, in hot oil, cook *half* of chops 10 minutes or until browned on both sides. Remove; set aside. Repeat with remaining chops. Pour off fat.

● In same skillet, combine *1 cup* tomato juice, onion, sugar, soy sauce, ginger and garlic powder. Heat to boiling. Return chops to skillet. Reduce heat to low. Cover; cook 5 minutes or until chops are no longer pink. Remove chops; keep warm.

● In small bowl, stir together cornstarch and remaining *¹/₂ cup* tomato juice until smooth. Add to skillet. Over medium heat, cook until mixture boils and thickens, stirring constantly. Spoon sauce over chops. Serve with pasta.

Serving Suggestion: Sweet 'n' Saucy Chops are served with hot cooked mostaccioli and steamed snow peas. Garnish with orange slices, fresh chives and edible flowers.

Makes 6 servings.
Prep Time: 5 minutes
Cook Time: 30 minutes

HERBED PORK CHOPS

2 tablespoons all-purpose flour

¹/₄ teaspoon ground sage

¹/₄ teaspoon dried thyme leaves, crushed

4 boneless pork chops, each ³/₄ inch thick (about 1 pound)

2 tablespoons margarine *or* butter

1 can (10 ³/₄ ounces) CAMPBELL'S condensed Cream of Chicken Soup

¹/₂ cup water

4 cups prepared long-grain and wild rice mix *or* hot cooked rice

● On waxed paper, combine flour, sage and thyme. Coat chops lightly with flour mixture.

● In 10-inch skillet over medium-high heat, in hot margarine, cook chops 10 minutes or until browned on both sides. Remove; set aside.

● In same skillet, combine soup and water. Heat to boiling. Return chops to skillet. Reduce heat to low. Cover; cook 5 minutes or until chops are no longer pink. Serve with rice.

Serving Suggestion: Herbed Pork Chops are served with rice and steamed green beans. Garnish with kumquat wedges, fresh thyme and edible flowers.

Makes 4 servings.
Prep Time: 5 minutes
Cook Time: 20 minutes

SPICY SHRIMP AND NOODLES

2 cups water

2 tablespoons soy sauce

1 teaspoon ground ginger

¹/₂ teaspoon crushed red pepper

¹/₄ teaspoon garlic powder

2 packages (3 ounces *each*) CAMPBELL'S Oriental Flavor or RAMEN PRIDE Chicken Flavor Ramen Noodle Soup

1 pound medium shrimp, shelled and deveined

1 cup frozen Oriental-style mixed vegetables

1 cup green onions cut in 2-inch pieces

Toasted sesame seeds *and* very thin strips of lemon and orange peel for garnish

● In 10-inch skillet over high heat, combine water, soy, ginger, red pepper, garlic and *half of one* seasoning packet. Heat to boiling. (Reserve remaining 1¹/₂ packets for another use.)

● Add noodles, shrimp, vegetables and onions. Return to boiling. Reduce heat to low. Cook 5 minutes or until shrimp turn pink and opaque and noodles are tender, stirring occasionally to separate noodles. Sprinkle with sesame seeds. Garnish with citrus peels, if desired.

TIP: If you're using fresh shrimp in shells, see tip, page 9, for shelling and deveining shrimp.

TIP: Cook shrimp quickly; overcooking toughens them. Cook shrimp just until they curl and the flesh turns pink and opaque.

Makes about 5 ¹/₂ cups or 4 servings.
Prep Time: 10 minutes
Cook Time: 15 minutes

SPICY SHRIMP AND NOODLES

CHEESY TUNA AND NOODLES

3 packages (3 ounces *each*)
CAMPBELL'S *or* RAMEN PRIDE
Chicken Flavor Ramen Noodle Soup

2 tablespoons margarine *or* butter

1 package (10 ounces) frozen mixed
vegetables, thawed and drained

$^1/_8$ teaspoon garlic powder *or* 1 clove
garlic, minced

1 can (10 $^3/_4$ ounces) CAMPBELL'S
condensed Cream of Mushroom Soup

1 $^1/_2$ cups shredded mozzarella cheese
(6 ounces)

$^3/_4$ cup milk

$^1/_8$ teaspoon pepper

Generous dash ground nutmeg

1 can (about 6 ounces) tuna, drained
and broken into chunks

● Prepare noodles according to package directions. Add seasoning packets; drain off most of liquid. Set aside.

● Meanwhile, in 10-inch skillet over medium heat, in hot margarine, cook vegetables and garlic powder 2 minutes or until vegetables are tender-crisp, stirring often.

● Add mushroom soup, cheese, milk, pepper and nutmeg. Cook until cheese is melted, stirring occasionally.

● Stir in reserved noodles and tuna. Heat through, stirring occasionally.

TIP: Canned tuna is packed in oil or water and is available three ways. *Solid-packed* canned tuna is the most expensive, and *flaked or grated* is the least expensive. *Chunk-style* is the most common and is moderately priced.

Makes about 7 cups or 6 servings.
Prep Time: 10 minutes
Cook Time: 20 minutes

SEAFOOD CHOWDER

1 tablespoon vegetable oil

1 large onion, chopped (about 1 cup)

$^3/_4$ teaspoon snipped fresh dill *or*
$^1/_4$ teaspoon dried dill weed, crushed

$^1/_8$ teaspoon garlic powder *or* 1 clove
garlic, minced

1 can (10 $^3/_4$ ounces) CAMPBELL'S
condensed Cream of Celery Soup

1 can (10 $^3/_4$ ounces) CAMPBELL'S
condensed Cream of Potato Soup

1 $^1/_2$ soup cans milk

$^1/_2$ pound medium shrimp, shelled and
deveined

$^1/_2$ pound firm white fish fillets, cut
into 2-inch pieces

Fresh dill sprig for garnish

● In 3-quart saucepan over medium heat, in hot oil, cook onion, snipped dill and garlic until onion is tender, stirring often.

● Stir in soups and milk. Heat to boiling, stirring often. Cook 8 minutes, stirring often. Reduce heat to low.

● Add shrimp and fish. Cook 5 minutes more or until shrimp turn pink and opaque and fish flakes easily when tested with fork, stirring often. Garnish with dill sprig, if desired.

TIP: If you're using fresh shrimp in shells, see tip, on page 9, for shelling and deveining shrimp.

Make about 6$^1/_2$ cups or 4 servings.
Prep Time: 15 minutes
Cook Time: 20 minutes

SHRIMP CREOLE

2 tablespoons margarine *or* butter

1 large green pepper, diced
  (about 1 cup)

2 ribs celery, thinly sliced
  (about 1 cup)

1 medium onion, chopped
  (about $1/2$ cup)

$1/2$ teaspoon dried oregano leaves,
  crushed

$1/4$ teaspoon garlic powder *or* 2 cloves
  garlic, minced

$1/8$ teaspoon ground red pepper
  (cayenne)

1 $1/2$ cups CAMPBELL'S Tomato Juice

1 tablespoon cornstarch

1 pound large shrimp, shelled and
  deveined

4 cups hot cooked parslied rice

Green onion brush for garnish

● In 10-inch skillet over medium heat, in hot margarine, cook green pepper, celery, onion, oregano, garlic powder and red pepper until vegetables are tender-crisp, stirring often.

● Add *1 cup* tomato juice. Heat to boiling. Reduce heat to low. Cover; cook 5 minutes, stirring occasionally.

● Meanwhile, in small bowl, stir together cornstarch and remaining *1/2 cup* tomato juice until smooth.

● Increase heat to medium. Add cornstarch mixture and shrimp to vegetable mixture. Cook until mixture boils and thickens and shrimp turn pink and opaque, stirring constantly. Serve over rice. Garnish with green onion, if desired.

TIP: If you're using fresh shrimp in shells, see tip, on page 9, for shelling and deveining shrimp.

Makes 4 cups shrimp mixture or 4 servings.
Prep Time: 20 minutes
Cook Time: 20 minutes

TIP: To store fresh shrimp, rinse them under cold running water; drain well. Refrigerate up to 2 days in a covered container. Or, store in the freezer up to 6 months in a covered container. For safety's sake, do not refreeze thawed shrimp.

SHRIMP CREOLE

ITALIAN CHICKEN AND PASTA

2 tablespoons olive oil

1 pound skinless, boneless chicken breasts, cut into 1-inch pieces

2 cups sliced fresh mushrooms (about 6 ounces)

1 large onion, diced (about 1 cup)

4 teaspoons cornstarch

2 cups CAMPBELL'S Tomato Juice

1/4 teaspoon dried basil leaves, crushed

1/8 teaspoon pepper

2 tablespoons snipped fresh parsley *or* 2 teaspoons dried parsley flakes

4 cups hot cooked linguine (about 8 ounces dry)

Fresh basil sprig for garnish

● In 10-inch skillet over medium-high heat, in *1 tablespoon* hot oil, cook *half* of the chicken until browned, stirring often. Remove; set aside. Repeat with remaining chicken.

● Reduce heat to medium. In same skillet, in remaining *1 tablespoon* hot oil, cook mushrooms and onion until vegetables are tender and liquid is evaporated, stirring often.

● In small bowl, stir together cornstarch, tomato juice, basil and pepper until smooth.

● Add cornstarch mixture to vegetable mixture. Cook until mixture boils and thickens, stirring constantly. Return chicken to skillet. Reduce heat to low. Cover; cook 5 minutes or until chicken is no longer pink, stirring occasionally. Stir in parsley. Serve over linguine. Sprinkle with additional snipped *fresh parsley*. Garnish with basil, if desired.

TIP: To snip fresh herbs, see tip, on page 8.

Makes about 4 cups or 4 main-dish servings.
Prep Time: 15 minutes
Cook Time: 20 minutes

ITALIAN CHICKEN AND PASTA

GARDEN CHICKEN LINGUINE

Vegetable cooking spray

1 pound skinless, boneless chicken breasts, cut into strips

1 can (26 ¹/₂ ounces) CAMPBELL'S Extra Garlic & Onion Spaghetti Sauce

1 bag (16 ounces) frozen vegetable combination (broccoli, carrots and cauliflower)

¹/₄ cup grated Parmesan cheese

¹/₄ teaspoon pepper

6 cups hot cooked linguine (about 12 ounces dry)

- Spray 10-inch skillet with cooking spray. Heat over medium-high heat 1 minute. Add *half* of the chicken; cook until browned, stirring often. Remove; set aside. Remove skillet from heat; spray with cooking spray. Repeat with remaining chicken.

- In same skillet, combine spaghetti sauce, vegetables, cheese and pepper. Heat to boiling. Reduce heat to low. Cover; cook 10 minutes or until vegetables are tender, stirring occasionally.

- Return chicken to skillet; heat through, stirring occasionally. Serve over linguine.

Makes about 6 cups or 6 main-dish servings.
Prep Time: 10 minutes
Cook Time: 25 minutes

ZESTY PASTA

¹/₂ pound ground beef

1 can (26 ¹/₂ ounces) CAMPBELL'S Extra Garlic & Onion Spaghetti Sauce

¹/₄ cup grated Parmesan cheese

¹/₄ teaspoon pepper

1 package (10 ounces) frozen chopped spinach, thawed and *well drained*

4 cups hot cooked corkscrew macaroni (about 3 cups dry)

- In 10-inch skillet over medium-high heat, cook beef until meat is browned, stirring to separate meat. Spoon off fat.

- Stir in spaghetti sauce, cheese and pepper. Heat to boiling. Reduce heat to low. Cover; cook 5 minutes, stirring occasionally.

- Stir in spinach. Serve *immediately* over hot macaroni.

TIP: Drain thawed spinach in colander. Press spinach with back of spoon to remove excess water.

Makes about 7 cups or 6 main-dish servings.
Prep Time: 10 minutes
Cook Time: 15 minutes

GARDEN CHICKEN LINGUINE

TURKEY TETRAZZINI

1 can (10 3/4 ounces) CAMPBELL'S
condensed Cream of Mushroom Soup

1/2 cup milk

1 small onion, finely chopped
(about 1/4 cup)

1/4 cup grated Parmesan cheese

1/4 cup sour cream

2 cans (5 ounces *each*) SWANSON
Premium Chunk White Turkey,
drained

1 small zucchini, cut in half lengthwise
and thinly sliced (about 1 cup)

1 1/2 cups cooked spaghetti
(3 ounces dry)

Toasted sliced almonds *and* fresh
tarragon sprig for garnish

● In large bowl, combine soup, milk, onion, cheese and sour cream. Stir in turkey and zucchini. Add spaghetti; toss gently to coat. Spoon into 1 1/2-quart casserole.

● Bake at 375°F. for 30 minutes or until hot and bubbling. Serve with additional grated *Parmesan cheese.* Garnish with almonds and tarragon, if desired.

TIP: Zucchini adds a fresh flavor to this creamy pasta and turkey main dish. When selecting zucchini, choose medium-size, firm ones; avoid those with soft spots on the skin.

Makes about 4 cups or 4 main-dish servings.
Prep Time: 20 minutes
Cook Time: 30 minutes

VEGETABLE LASAGNA

**4 medium carrots, shredded
(about 2 cups)**

**2 medium zucchini, chopped
(about 2 cups)**

1 cup ricotta cheese

Vegetable cooking spray

9 cooked lasagna noodles

**1 can (26 ¹/₂ ounces) CAMPBELL'S
Mushroom & Garlic Spaghetti Sauce**

**1 cup shredded mozzarella cheese
(4 ounces)**

● In large bowl, combine carrots, zucchini and ricotta cheese; set aside.

● Spray 3-quart oblong baking dish with cooking spray. In baking dish, arrange *three* lasagna noodles; spread with *half* of the cheese mixture. Top with *one-third* of the spaghetti sauce. Repeat layers. Top with remaining *three* lasagna noodles and remaining *one-third* spaghetti sauce. Sprinkle with the mozzarella cheese.

● Bake at 400°F. for 30 minutes or until hot and bubbling. Let stand 10 minutes before serving.

Makes 6 main-dish servings.
Prep Time: 25 minutes
Cook Time: 30 minutes
Stand Time: 10 minutes

EXTRA-EASY LASAGNA

³/₄ pound ground beef

3 cups PREGO Traditional Spaghetti Sauce

6 *uncooked* lasagna noodles

1 container (15 ounces) ricotta cheese (about 2 cups)

2 cups shredded mozzarella cheese (8 ounces)

¹/₄ cup water

Salad greens *and* cherry tomatoes for garnish

● In 10-inch skillet over medium-high heat, cook beef until browned, stirring to separate meat. Spoon off fat. Add spaghetti sauce; heat through, stirring occasionally.

● In 2-quart oblong baking dish, spread *1 ¹/₂ cups* meat mixture. Top with *three uncooked* lasagna noodles, *half* of the ricotta cheese and *half* of the mozzarella cheese. Repeat layers. Top with remaining meat mixture. Slowly pour water around *inside edges* of baking dish. Cover tightly with foil.

● Bake at 375°F. for 45 minutes. Uncover; bake 10 minutes more. Let stand 10 minutes before serving. Garnish each serving with salad greens and tomatoes, if desired.

Makes 8 main-dish servings.
Prep Time: 10 minutes
Cook Time: 65 minutes
Stand Time: 10 minutes

1 Stir in spaghetti sauce; heat to boiling.

EXTRA-EASY LASAGNA

2 In 2-quart oblong baking dish, spread *1 1/2 cups* meat mixture.

3 Top *uncooked* lasagna noodles with *half* of the ricotta cheese and *half* of the mozzarella cheese. Repeat layers.

4 Pour 1/4 cup water around *inside edges* of baking dish.

ℋAM AND PASTA SKILLET

1 can (10 ³/₄ ounces) CAMPBELL'S condensed Broccoli Cheese Soup

1 cup milk

1 tablespoon spicy brown mustard

2 cups fresh broccoli flowerets *or* frozen broccoli cuts

3 cups cooked medium shell macaroni (about 2 cups dry)

1 ¹/₂ cups cooked ham cut in thin strips (8 ounces)

Thin strips sweet red pepper for garnish

● In 10-inch skillet, combine soup, milk and mustard. Add broccoli. Over medium heat, heat to boiling, stirring occasionally. Reduce heat to low. Cover; cook 5 minutes or until broccoli is tender.

● Add macaroni and ham. Heat through, stirring occasionally. Garnish with red pepper, if desired.

Chicken and Pasta Skillet: Prepare Ham and Pasta Skillet as directed above, *except* substitute 2 tablespoons *Dijon-style mustard* for the spicy brown mustard, 3 cups cooked *radiatore pasta* (about 2 cups dry) for the shell macaroni and 1 ¹/₂ cups *cooked chicken strips* for the ham.

TIP: You can store dried pasta in a closed package in a cool, dry area indefinitely. Store fresh or refrigerated pasta in an airtight container in the refrigerator for up to 5 days or in the freezer up to 8 months.

Makes about 6 cups or 4 main-dish servings.
Prep Time: 20 minutes
Cook Time: 15 minutes

HAM AND PASTA SKILLET

GREEK-STYLE BEEF 'N' MAC BAKE

$1/2$ pound ground beef

1 medium onion, chopped
  (about $1/2$ cup)

$1/4$ teaspoon ground cinnamon

$1/4$ teaspoon pepper

1 $1/2$ cups CAMPBELL'S Tomato Juice

1 can (10 $3/4$ ounces) CAMPBELL'S condensed Golden Mushroom Soup

$1/2$ cup milk

$1/4$ cup grated Parmesan cheese

1 egg, slightly beaten

3 cups cooked elbow macaroni
  (about 1 $1/2$ cups dry)

Cherry tomato wedges, VLASIC *or*
  EARLY CALIFORNIA Pitted Ripe Olives,
  sliced, *and* fresh parsley sprig for
  garnish

● In 10-inch skillet over medium-high heat, cook beef, onion and cinnamon until beef is browned and onion is tender, stirring to separate meat. Spoon off fat.

● Stir in tomato juice. Heat to boiling. Reduce heat to low; cook 5 minutes. Spoon into 8- by 8-inch baking dish.

● In medium bowl, combine soup, milk, Parmesan cheese and egg. Add macaroni; toss to coat. Spoon over beef mixture.

● Bake at 350°F. for 30 minutes or until hot and bubbling and center is set. Let stand 10 minutes before serving. Garnish with tomato, olives and parsley, if desired.

Makes 4 main-dish servings.
Prep Time: 20 minutes
Cook Time: 30 minutes
Stand Time: 10 minutes

GREEK-STYLE BEEF 'N' MAC BAKE

1 In 10-inch skillet, cook beef, onion and cinnamon until beef is browned and onion is tender, stirring to separate meat.

2 In bowl, combine soup, milk, cheese and egg. Add macaroni; toss to coat.

3 Spoon macaroni mixture over beef mixture in baking dish.

RAVIOLI AND SAUSAGE

1/2 pound sweet Italian pork sausage, casing removed

3 cups PREGO EXTRA CHUNKY Mushroom & Green Pepper Spaghetti Sauce

1 package (about 14 ounces) frozen cheese-filled ravioli, cooked and drained

Grated Parmesan cheese *and* fresh oregano sprigs for garnish

● In 10-inch skillet over medium-high heat, cook sausage until browned and no longer pink, stirring to separate meat. Spoon off fat.

● Stir in spaghetti sauce. Heat to boiling. Add ravioli. Heat through, stirring occasionally. Sprinkle with cheese. Garnish with oregano, if desired.

TIP: Keep frozen pasta in the freezer for up to 8 months.

Makes 4 main-dish servings.
Prep Time: 10 minutes
Cook Time: 15 minutes

CHEDDAR-BROCCOLI NOODLES

4 cups water

2 packages (3 ounces each) CAMPBELL'S *or* RAMEN PRIDE Chicken Flavor Ramen Noodle Soup

1 ¹/₂ cups fresh broccoli flowerets

1 can (10 ³/₄ ounces) CAMPBELL'S condensed Cheddar Cheese Soup

¹/₄ cup sour cream *or* plain yogurt

¹/₈ teaspoon pepper

Very thin strips sweet red pepper for garnish

● In 3-quart saucepan over high heat, heat water to boiling. Add noodles and broccoli. Return to boiling. Reduce heat to low. Cover; cook 5 minutes or until noodles and broccoli are tender, stirring occasionally to separate noodles.

● Stir in *one* seasoning packet; drain off most of liquid. (Reserve remaining seasoning packet for another use.)

● Add cheese soup, sour cream and pepper. Heat through, stirring occasionally. Garnish with sweet red pepper, if desired.

Makes about 4 cups or 6 side-dish servings.
Prep Time: 10 minutes
Cook Time: 15 minutes

CHEDDARY PASTA AND VEGETABLES

1 1/2 cups dry corkscrew macaroni

1 cup fresh broccoli flowerets

2 medium carrots, sliced (about 1 cup)

1 large sweet red *or* green pepper, coarsely chopped (about 1 cup), optional

1 can (10 3/4 ounces) CAMPBELL'S condensed Cream of Celery Soup

1/2 cup shredded Cheddar cheese (2 ounces)

1/2 cup milk

1 tablespoon prepared mustard

- In 4-quart saucepan, prepare macaroni according to package directions. Add broccoli, carrots and red pepper for last 5 minutes of cooking time. Drain in colander.

- In same saucepan, combine soup, cheese, milk and mustard. Over low heat, heat until cheese is melted, stirring often.

- Add macaroni and vegetables. Heat through, stirring occasionally.

Makes about 4 1/2 cups or 5 side-dish servings.
Prep Time: 10 minutes
Cook Time: 20 minutes

BROCCOLI AND NOODLES SUPREME

3 cups dry medium egg noodles

2 cups fresh broccoli flowerets

1 can (10 3/4 ounces) CAMPBELL'S condensed Cream of Chicken & Broccoli Soup

1/2 cup sour cream

1/3 cup grated Parmesan cheese

1/8 teaspoon pepper

- In 4-quart saucepan, prepare noodles according to package directions. Add broccoli for last 5 minutes of cooking time. Drain.

- In same saucepan, combine soup, sour cream, cheese and pepper; add noodles and broccoli. Over low heat, heat through, stirring occasionally.

- Sprinkle with additional grated *Parmesan cheese* and *freshly ground pepper*, if desired.

Makes about 4 cups or 5 side-dish servings.
Prep Time: 5 minutes
Cook Time: 20 minutes

CHEDDARY PASTA AND VEGETABLES

TOMATO-BASIL PASTA SAUCE

1 can (10 ³/₄ ounces) CAMPBELL'S
  condensed Broccoli Cheese Soup

³/₄ cup half-and-half *or* milk

3 fresh plum tomatoes, coarsely
  chopped (about 1 cup) *or* 4 canned
  plum tomatoes, drained and coarsely
  chopped (about ³/₄ cup)

¹/₄ cup grated Parmesan cheese

1 tablespoon snipped fresh basil leaves
  or 1 teaspoon dried basil leaves,
  crushed

3 cups hot cooked fettuccine (about
  6 ounces dry)

Toasted pine nuts *and* fresh basil sprig
  for garnish

● In 2-quart saucepan, combine soup, half-and-half, tomatoes, cheese and snipped basil. Over medium heat, heat to boiling. Reduce heat to low; cook 5 minutes, stirring often.

● Pour over fettuccine; toss gently to coat. Sprinkle with pine nuts. Garnish with basil, if desired.

TIP: You can also serve this pasta sauce over hot cooked linguine, spaghetti or fusilli.

Makes about 2 ¹/₂ cups or 4 side-dish servings.
Prep Time: 20 minutes
Cook Time: 10 minutes

CHEESY VEGETABLE MACARONI

1 tablespoon olive *or* vegetable oil

2 medium zucchini, sliced
(about 3 cups)

1 can (26 ¹/₂ ounces) CAMPBELL'S
Mushroom & Garlic Spaghetti Sauce

¹/₄ cup grated Parmesan cheese

4 cups hot cooked corkscrew macaroni
(about 3 cups dry)

1 cup shredded mozzarella cheese
(4 ounces)

● In 10-inch skillet over medium heat, in hot oil, cook zucchini until tender-crisp, stirring occasionally.

● Add spaghetti sauce and Parmesan cheese. Heat to boiling. Reduce heat to low. Cover; cook 5 minutes, stirring occasionally.

● Toss pasta-vegetable sauce with macaroni. Sprinkle with mozzarella cheese.

Makes about 6 cups or 6 side-dish servings.
Prep Time: 10 minutes
Cook Time: 15 minutes

ITALIAN VEGETABLES AND PASTA

1 tablespoon olive *or* vegetable oil

2 medium carrots, thinly sliced
   (about 1 cup)

1 medium zucchini, sliced
   (about 1 ¹/₂ cups)

1 medium onion, sliced and separated
   into rings (about ¹/₂ cup)

1 cup CAMPBELL'S Tomato Juice

¹/₄ cup grated Parmesan cheese

¹/₄ teaspoon dried oregano leaves,
   crushed

¹/₄ teaspoon garlic powder *or* 2 cloves
   garlic, minced

2 cups cooked pasta (ziti, rotelle or
   medium shell *or* corkscrew macaroni)

Fresh oregano sprig for garnish

● In 10-inch skillet over medium heat, in hot oil, cook carrots, zucchini and onion until vegetables are tender-crisp, stirring often.

● Add tomato juice, cheese, oregano and garlic powder. Heat to boiling. Reduce heat to low. Cover; cook 5 minutes or until vegetables are tender, stirring occasionally.

● Add pasta. Heat through, stirring occasionally. Garnish with oregano, if desired.

Makes about 4 cups or 4 side-dish servings.
Prep Time: 15 minutes
Cook Time: 10 minutes

SPAGHETTI PIE

1 ³/₄ cups PREGO Traditional Spaghetti
   Sauce

2 eggs, beaten

4 cups hot cooked spaghetti
   (about 8 ounces dry)

1 cup ricotta cheese

3 tablespoons snipped fresh parsley *or*
   1 tablespoon dried parsley flakes

2 tablespoons grated Parmesan cheese

● Reserve ¹/₃ *cup* spaghetti sauce; set aside. In medium bowl, combine remaining spaghetti sauce and eggs. Add spaghetti; toss to coat well.

● In 9-inch pie plate, evenly spread spaghetti mixture.

● In small bowl, combine ricotta cheese and parsley. Spread evenly on spaghetti shell to within *1 inch of edge*. Top with reserved spaghetti sauce; sprinkle with Parmesan cheese.

● Bake at 350°F. for 30 minutes. Let stand 5 minutes before serving. Cut into wedges.

Makes 6 side-dish servings.
Prep Time: 15 minutes
Cook Time: 30 minutes
Stand Time: 5 minutes

ITALIAN VEGETABLES AND PASTA

$\mathcal{V}$EGETABLE ROTINI

2 $^1/_2$ cups dry rotini *or* corkscrew macaroni

1 $^1/_2$ cups fresh broccoli flowerets

1 $^1/_2$ cups fresh cauliflowerets

2 medium carrots, cut into strips (about 1 cup)

1 can (10 $^3/_4$ ounces) CAMPBELL'S condensed Broccoli Cheese Soup

1 package (3 ounces) cream cheese *or* cream cheese with chives, softened

$^3/_4$ cup milk

$^1/_2$ cup grated Parmesan cheese

2 tablespoons Dijon-style mustard (optional)

$^1/_8$ teaspoon pepper

● In 4-quart saucepan, prepare rotini according to package directions. Add broccoli, cauliflower and carrots for last 5 minutes of cooking time. Drain in colander.

● In same saucepan, gradually stir soup into cream cheese; add milk, Parmesan cheese, mustard and pepper. Over low heat, heat until cream cheese is melted, stirring often. Add macaroni and vegetables. Heat through, stirring occasionally.

TIP: You may substitute 1 bag (16 ounces) frozen vegetable combination (such as broccoli, cauliflower and carrots) for the fresh vegetables.

Makes about 6 cups or 6 side-dish servings.
Prep Time: 10 minutes
Cook Time: 25 minutes

MUSHROOM-BROCCOLI ALFREDO

2 tablespoons margarine *or* butter

3 cups fresh broccoli flowerets

3 cups sliced fresh mushrooms
(about 8 ounces)

1 medium onion, coarsely chopped
(about $^1/_2$ cup)

$^1/_4$ teaspoon garlic powder *or* 2 cloves
garlic, minced

1 can (10 $^3/_4$ ounces) CAMPBELL'S
condensed Cream of Mushroom Soup

$^1/_3$ cup milk *or* Chablis or other dry
white wine

2 tablespoons grated Parmesan cheese

$^1/_8$ teaspoon pepper

4 cups hot cooked fettuccine *or*
spaghetti (about 8 ounces dry)

● In 10-inch skillet over medium heat, in hot margarine, cook broccoli, mushrooms, onion and garlic until vegetables are tender-crisp and liquid is evaporated, stirring often.

● Add soup, milk, cheese and pepper. Heat through, stirring occasionally. Serve over fettuccine. Sprinkle with additional grated *Parmesan cheese*, if desired.

Serving Suggestion: Mushroom-Broccoli Alfredo is served over hot cooked fettuccine, along with Baked Onion Chicken (*see recipe, page 55*). Garnish with cherry tomato and fresh oregano.

Makes about 3 cups or 4 side-dish servings.
Prep Time: 10 minutes
Cook Time: 25 minutes

BISTRO CHICKEN SALAD

4 skinless, boneless chicken breast halves (about 1 pound)

1 jar (12 ounces) refrigerated MARIE'S Honey Mustard Dressing and Dip

1 1/2 cups PEPPERIDGE FARM Homestyle Sourdough Cheese Croutons, crushed

Mixed salad greens torn into bite-size pieces

2 tablespoons orange juice

2 teaspoons grated orange peel

Orange slices *and* edible flowers for garnish

● In shallow dish, dip chicken into *1/2 cup dressing*. On waxed paper, coat chicken with croutons.

● On baking sheet, arrange chicken. Bake at 400°F. for 20 minutes or until chicken is no longer pink.

● Cut each breast half into strips. Arrange on salad greens.

● In 1-quart saucepan, combine orange juice, orange peel and remaining dressing. Over medium heat, heat through. Drizzle over chicken. Garnish with orange slices and edible flowers, if desired.

TIP: To microwave dressing, in small microwave-safe bowl, stir orange juice, orange peel and remaining dressing. Microwave on HIGH 30 seconds; stir. Drizzle over chicken.

Makes 4 main-dish servings.
Prep Time: 10 minutes
Cook Time: 20 minutes

TIP: Edible flowers are an easy and colorful way to garnish salads, soups, beverages and desserts. Not all flowers are edible. Purchase edible flowers at specialty produce markets or supermarkets that carry gourmet produce. Do not use flowers from florist shops; they are usually treated with chemicals. Before using, rinse flowers and gently pat dry. Store edible flowers in an airtight container in the refrigerator up to one week. Pictured here is "borage," a purple-blue flower with a cucumber-like flavor. Other popular edible flowers include: nasturtiums, chive blossoms, pansies and roses.

BISTRO CHICKEN SALAD

ORIENTAL BEEF SALAD

²/₃ cup refrigerated **MARIE'S ZESTY Fat Free Red Wine Vinaigrette**

1 tablespoon soy sauce

1 teaspoon sesame oil

2 cups sliced fresh mushrooms (about 6 ounces)

1 medium sweet yellow *or* red pepper, cut into strips (about 1 cup)

2 medium green onions, sliced (about ¹/₄ cup)

³/₄ pound beef top round steak (1 inch thick)

2 cups mixed salad greens torn in bite-size pieces

● In medium bowl, combine vinaigrette, soy sauce and sesame oil. Reserve *2 tablespoons*; set aside.

● Add mushrooms, yellow pepper and onions to remaining vinaigrette mixture; toss to coat. Set aside.

● Brush both sides of steak with reserved *2 tablespoons* vinaigrette mixture. On rack in broiler pan, arrange steak. Broil 4 inches from heat until desired doneness (allow 18 minutes for medium, 160°F.), turning once during cooking.

● Thinly slice steak. On 4 plates, arrange salad greens. Divide steak and vegetables evenly among the 4 plates.

Makes 4 main-dish servings.
Prep Time: 10 minutes
Cook Time: 20 minutes

1 To clean mushrooms, wipe lightly with a damp cloth. Or, brush lightly with a soft brush.

ORIENTAL BEEF SALAD

2 Trim a thin slice off stem end; cut mushrooms into slices.

3 Slice off stem end of pepper; cut pepper in half from top to bottom. Remove membrane and seeds; discard. Rinse and drain pepper. Stack pepper halves on top of each other. Slice into thin strips.

4 Arrange cooked steak slices on salad greens.

TORTELLINI SALAD

8 ounces frozen cheese-filled tortellini (about 2 cups)

¹/₂ cup refrigerated MARIE'S ZESTY Fat Free Italian Vinaigrette

1 small cucumber, diced (about 1 cup)

1 medium tomato, diced (about 1 cup)

1 medium green onion, sliced (about 2 tablespoons)

Leaf lettuce (optional)

Fresh oregano sprigs *and* cherry tomatoes for garnish

● Cook tortellini according to package directions. Drain in colander. In medium bowl, toss hot tortellini with vinaigrette; cool 10 minutes.

● Add cucumber, tomato and onion; toss gently to coat. Serve at room temperature or cover and refrigerate until serving time. Serve on lettuce-lined plate. Garnish with oregano and tomatoes, if desired.

TIP: You may substitute refrigerated MARIE'S ZESTY Fat Free Red Wine Vinaigrette for the Italian Vinaigrette.

Makes 4 1/2 cups or 4 main-dish servings.
Prep Time: 30 minutes

CHICKEN AND PASTA SALAD

3/4 cup refrigerated MARIE'S Creamy
   Ranch Dressing and Dip

18 medium cherry tomatoes, halved
   (about 1 1/2 cups)

1 medium cucumber, peeled, halved
   lengthwise, seeded and sliced
   (about 1 1/3 cups)

2 thin wedges red onion, separated
   (about 1/4 cup)

3 tablespoons snipped fresh parsley *or*
   1 tablespoon dried parsley flakes

2 cans (5 ounces *each*) SWANSON
   Premium Chunk White Chicken,
   drained

3 cups cooked corkscrew macaroni
   (about 2 1/2 cups dry)

● In large bowl, combine salad dressing, tomatoes, cucumber, onion and parsley.

● Add chicken and pasta; toss gently to coat. Cover; refrigerate at least 4 hours before serving.

Makes about 7 cups or 5 main-dish servings.
Prep Time: 20 minutes
Chill Time: 4 hours

CHINESE CHICKEN SALAD

8 ounces dry spaghetti *or* vermicelli, broken into thirds

$1/3$ cup water

3 tablespoons creamy peanut butter

2 tablespoons soy sauce

$1/8$ teaspoon crushed red pepper

1 cup snow peas cut diagonally in 1-inch pieces (about 4 ounces)

2 cans (5 ounces *each*) SWANSON Premium Chunk White Chicken, drained

$1/2$ cup sweet red *or* green pepper strips

3 medium green onions, sliced (about $1/3$ cup)

3 cups shredded spinach leaves (about 4 ounces)

Fresh shiitake mushrooms for garnish

- Cook spaghetti according to package directions. Drain in colander.

- Meanwhile, in 1-quart saucepan, combine water, peanut butter, soy sauce and crushed red pepper. Over medium heat, heat to boiling, stirring constantly.

- Add snow peas; cook until sauce is smooth and peas are tender-crisp, stirring constantly.

- In large bowl, combine hot spaghetti, chicken, red pepper strips and green onions. Pour sauce mixture over spaghetti mixture; toss to coat. Serve immediately on spinach. Garnish with mushrooms, if desired.

Makes about 6 cups or 6 main-dish servings.
Prep Time: 20 minutes

CHINESE CHICKEN SALAD

GARDEN CHICKEN SALAD

2 cups mixed salad greens torn in bite-size pieces

1 can (5 ounces) SWANSON Premium Chunk White Chicken, drained

1 hard-cooked egg, sliced

1 small green pepper, cut into rings

1 small tomato, cut into 6 wedges

4 red onion rings

$1/4$ cup VLASIC *or* EARLY CALIFORNIA pitted ripe olives

$1/4$ cup refrigerated MARIE'S Thousand Island Dressing and Dip

PEPPERIDGE FARM Sesame Thin Bread Sticks (optional)

● On 2 plates, arrange salad greens. Divide chicken, egg, green pepper, tomato, onion and olives between plates.

● Drizzle with dressing. Serve with bread sticks, if desired.

Makes 2 main-dish servings.
Prep Time: 15 minutes

1 Whack core end of iceberg lettuce on work surface. Pull and twist out core.

GARDEN CHICKEN SALAD

2 Wash lettuce; dry in salad spinner or gently pat dry with paper towels. Tear into bite-size pieces.

3 Cut lengthwise along both sides of the thick midrib of romaine leaves; remove and discard. Tear into bite-size pieces.

4 Slice stem and bottom ends off pepper. Remove membrane and seeds; discard. Rinse and drain pepper. Slice pepper cross-wise into rings.

TACO SALAD

1 pound ground beef

2 tablespoons chili powder

1 pouch CAMPBELL'S Dry Onion Soup and Recipe Mix

$1/2$ cup water

6 cups torn leaf lettuce

Tortilla chips

1 medium tomato, chopped (about 1 cup)

1 cup shredded Cheddar cheese (4 ounces)

Fresh parsley sprigs *and* VLASIC Cherry Peppers for garnish

● In 10-inch skillet over medium heat, cook beef and chili powder until browned and no longer pink, stirring to separate meat. Spoon off fat.

● Stir in soup mix and water. Heat to boiling. Reduce heat to low. Cook 10 minutes, stirring occasionally.

● Arrange lettuce and tortilla chips on plates. Spoon hot meat mixture over chips. Top with tomatoes and cheese. Garnish with parsley and cherry peppers, if desired.

Tacos: Prepare meat mixture for Taco Salad as directed above. Spoon about $1/4$ *cup* of meat mixture into each of *12 warm taco shells*. Top with lettuce, tomato and cheese.

Makes 6 main-dish servings.
Prep Time: 10 minutes
Cook Time: 15 minutes

LENTIL-RICE SALAD

2 cups water

¹/₂ cup dry lentils

¹/₂ cup uncooked regular long-grain rice

1 rib celery, sliced (about ¹/₂ cup)

¹/₂ cup chopped red onion

¹/₂ cup sweet yellow *or* green pepper strips

2 tablespoons snipped fresh parsley

¹/₂ cup refrigerated MARIE'S ZESTY Fat Free White Wine Vinaigrette

Generous dash ground red pepper (cayenne)

Lettuce leaves

Fresh parsley sprigs for garnish

PEPPERIDGE FARM Cheddar Cheese Thin Bread Sticks

● In 2-quart saucepan over high heat, heat water to boiling. Stir in lentils and rice; return to boiling. Reduce heat to low. Cover; cook 20 minutes or until lentils and rice are tender. Remove from heat. Let stand, covered, 5 minutes or until liquid is absorbed.

● In medium bowl, combine lentil mixture, celery, onion, yellow pepper strips and snipped parsley. Add vinaigrette and red pepper; toss to coat.

● Cover; refrigerate at least 4 hours before serving. Serve on lettuce. Garnish with parsley, if desired. Serve with bread sticks, if desired.

Makes about 4 cups or 8 side-dish servings.
Prep Time: 35 minutes
Chill Time: 4 hours

CAESAR BEAN SALAD

1 can (16 ounces) chick peas
(garbanzo beans), rinsed and drained

1 can (about 15 ounces) kidney beans,
rinsed and drained

$^1/_2$ cup refrigerated MARIE'S Creamy
Caesar Dressing and Dip

4 thin wedges red onion, separated
(about $^1/_2$ cup)

$^1/_2$ cup snipped fresh parsley

● In medium bowl, combine chick peas, kidney beans, dressing, onion and parsley; toss to coat. Serve immediately. Or, cover and refrigerate until serving time.

Serving Suggestion: On platter, arrange Belgian endive leaves and large fresh basil leaves. Top with Caesar Bean Salad. Garnish with cherry tomato wedges and fresh chives.

Makes about 4 cups or 8 side-dish servings.
Prep Time: 15 minutes

GLAZED FRUIT SALAD

1 can (about 11 ounces) mandarin orange segments, drained

1 cup seedless green *or* red grapes

1 cup sliced fresh strawberries

2 medium bananas, sliced

1 medium apple, cored and diced

1/2 cup MARIE'S Creamy Glaze for Bananas

● In large bowl, combine fruit and glaze; toss to coat. Serve immediately. Or, cover and refrigerate until serving time.

Coconut-Marshmallow Fruit Salad: Prepare Glazed Fruit Salad as directed above, *except*, just before serving, gently stir in 1/2 cup *miniature marshmallows*. Sprinkle with 1/4 cup *flaked coconut*. Makes about 5 1/2 cups.

Makes about 5 cups or 5 side-dish servings.
Prep Time: 15 minutes

SKILLET ROSEMARY POTATOES

1 tablespoon margarine *or* butter

1 ¹/₂ cups quartered fresh mushrooms
(about 4 ounces)

1 medium onion, chopped
(about ¹/₂ cup)

¹/₄ teaspoon dried rosemary leaves,
crushed

1 can (10 ¹/₂ ounces)
FRANCO-AMERICAN Mushroom Gravy

4 medium red potatoes
(about 1 ¹/₄ pounds), quartered
(about 4 cups)

Green onion brush for garnish

● In 10-inch skillet over medium heat, in hot margarine, cook mushrooms, onion and rosemary until vegetables are tender and liquid is evaporated, stirring often.

● Add gravy and potatoes. Heat to boiling. Reduce heat to low. Cover; cook 20 minutes or until potatoes are tender, stirring occasionally. Garnish with green onion, if desired.

Makes about 4 3/4 cups or 6 servings.
Prep Time: 10 minutes
Cook Time: 30 minutes

CHEDDAR-POTATO BAKE

1 can (10 ³/₄ ounces) CAMPBELL'S
condensed Cheddar Cheese Soup

¹/₃ cup sour cream *or* plain yogurt

1 medium green onion, chopped
(about 2 tablespoons)

Generous dash pepper

3 cups stiff seasoned mashed potatoes

● In 2-quart saucepan, combine soup, sour cream, onion and pepper. Stir in potatoes until blended. Over low heat, heat through, stirring often.

TIP: This recipe can also be baked in the oven. In 1 1/2-quart casserole, combine soup, sour cream, onion and pepper. Stir in potatoes until blended. Bake at 350°F. for 30 minutes or until hot.

Makes about 4 ¹/₂ cups or 8 servings.
Prep Time: 10 minutes
Cook Time: 15 minutes

SKILLET ROSEMARY POTATOES

*N*EW POTATOES AND PEAS

9 small new potatoes, quartered (about 1 ¹/₂ pounds)

1 can (10 ³/₄ ounces) CAMPBELL'S condensed Cream of Mushroom Soup

¹/₃ cup milk

¹/₂ teaspoon dried dill weed *or* thyme leaves, crushed

¹/₈ teaspoon pepper

1 package (10 ounces) frozen peas with pearl onions *or* peas, thawed and drained

Fresh dill sprigs for garnish

● In 4-quart saucepan, place potatoes. Add water to cover potatoes. Over high heat, heat to boiling. Reduce heat to medium. Cook 8 minutes or until potatoes are fork-tender. Drain in colander.

● In same saucepan, combine soup, milk, dried dill and pepper. Add potatoes and peas with pearl onions. Over low heat, heat through, stirring occasionally. Garnish with fresh dill, if desired.

Makes about 5 ¹/₂ cups or 7 servings.
Prep Time: 5 minutes
Cook Time: 20 minutes

BROCCOLI-CHEESE POTATO TOPPER

1 can (10 ¾ ounces) CAMPBELL'S condensed Cream of Celery Soup

1 teaspoon Dijon-style mustard

⅛ teaspoon pepper

2 cups cooked broccoli flowerets

½ cup shredded Cheddar *or* Swiss cheese (2 ounces)

4 hot baked potatoes, split lengthwise

Fresh parsley sprigs for garnish

● In 2-quart saucepan, combine soup, mustard and pepper. Over low heat, heat through, stirring often. Add broccoli and cheese. Heat through, stirring often. Serve over potatoes. Garnish with parsley, if desired.

TIP: For oven-baked potatoes, scrub 4 potatoes (8 ounces each); pierce each potato with fork several times. Bake at 400°F. for 1 hour or until fork-tender.

TIP: For micro-cooked potatoes, scrub 4 potatoes (8 ounces each); pierce each potato with fork several times. Arrange potatoes in circle on microwave-safe plate. Microwave, uncovered, on HIGH for 10 to 12 minutes, rearranging potatoes once during cooking. Let stand a few minutes before serving.

Makes about 2 cups or 4 side-dish servings.
Prep Time: 10 minutes
Cook Time: 10 minutes

GLAZED VEGETABLES

2 tablespoons cornstarch

1 can (14 ¹/₂ ounces) SWANSON Ready
   To Serve Clear Vegetable Broth

1 tablespoon vegetable oil

2 medium carrots, sliced (about 1 cup)

2 ribs celery, sliced (about 1 cup)

1 medium sweet red pepper, cut into
   strips (about 1 cup)

1 large onion, cut into wedges
   (about 1 cup)

¹/₂ teaspoon ground ginger

¹/₄ teaspoon garlic powder *or* 2 cloves
   garlic, minced

1 cup fresh broccoli flowerets

1 cup fresh snow peas
   (about 4 ounces), trimmed

● In small bowl, stir together cornstarch and broth until smooth; set aside.

● In 10-inch skillet or wok over medium heat, in hot oil, stir-fry carrots, celery, red pepper, onion, ginger and garlic powder until vegetables are tender-crisp.

● Add broccoli and snow peas. Add reserved broth mixture. Cook until mixture boils and thickens, stirring constantly.

● Reduce heat to low. Cover; cook until vegetables are tender, stirring occasionally.

TIP: Celery grows in bunches called stalks. Each stalk consists of many "ribs" with leafy green tops. The tender center is commonly referred to as the "heart."

Makes about 4 cups or 4 servings.
Prep Time: 15 minutes
Cook Time: 15 minutes

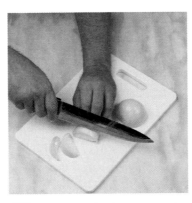

1 Cut peeled onion in half from stem to root end. Place cut sides down on cutting board. Cut each half lengthwise into 4 to 6 wedges.

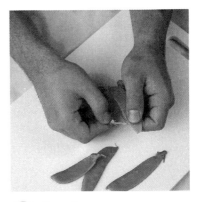

2 Gently remove stem end of snow peas without breaking the string. Pull string down entire pod; discard string.

GLAZED VEGETABLES

3 In bowl, stir together cornstarch and broth until smooth.

4 In wok over medium heat, in hot oil, stir-fry vegetables, ginger and garlic until vegetables are tender-crisp.

5 Add broth mixture.

Cinnamon Carrots

1 teaspoon cornstarch

1 cup CAMPBELL'S Tomato Juice

3 tablespoons packed brown sugar

1/2 teaspoon ground cinnamon

1 package (about 16 ounces) frozen
baby carrots, cooked and drained

Fresh parsley sprig for garnish

● In 2-quart saucepan, stir together corn-starch, tomato juice, brown sugar and cinna-mon until smooth. Over medium heat, cook until mixture boils and thickens, stirring con-stantly. Add carrots. Heat through, stirring occasionally.

● Garnish with parsley, if desired.

Makes about 2 1/2 cups or 4 servings.
Prep Time: 5 minutes
Cook Time: 15 minutes

Saucy Asparagus

1 can (10 3/4 ounces) CAMPBELL'S
condensed Cream of Asparagus Soup

2 tablespoons milk

1 1/2 pounds fresh asparagus spears
(24 to 30), trimmed and cut into
1-inch pieces (about 3 cups), *or*
2 packages (10 ounces each) frozen
asparagus cuts

Cherry tomato wedges *and* fresh
oregano sprig for garnish

● In 2-quart saucepan, combine soup and milk. Over medium heat, heat to boiling, stirring occasionally.

● Add asparagus. Reduce heat to low. Cover; cook 10 minutes or until asparagus is tender, stirring occasionally. Garnish with tomato and oregano, if desired.

Makes about 3 cups or 6 servings.
Prep Time: 10 minutes
Cook Time: 15 minutes

CINNAMON CARROTS (TOP)
SAUCY ASPARAGUS (BOTTOM)

GLAZED SWEET POTATOES

4 cans (about 23 ounces *each*) whole sweet potatoes in syrup, drained

1 container (14 ounces) MARIE'S Glaze for Peaches

¹/₄ cup chopped pecans *or* walnuts

¹/₂ teaspoon vanilla extract

Fresh parsley sprig *and* apple slices for garnish

● In 3-quart oblong baking dish, arrange sweet potatoes. In small bowl, combine glaze, walnuts and vanilla; spoon evenly over potatoes.

● Bake at 350°F. for 30 minutes or until hot and bubbling, stirring once during baking. Garnish with parsley and apple, if desired.

TIP: You may substitute 12 medium sweet potatoes (about 6 pounds), cooked, peeled and quartered for the canned sweet potatoes.

TIP: You may substitute 4 cans (about 16 ounces each) *vacuum-packed* sweet potatoes, drained, for the canned sweet potatoes in syrup.

Makes about 8 ¹/₂ cups or 12 servings.
Prep Time: 5 minutes
Cook Time: 30 minutes

CLASSIC GREEN BEAN BAKE

1 can (10 ³/₄ ounces) CAMPBELL'S
condensed Cream of Mushroom Soup

¹/₂ cup milk

1 teaspoon soy sauce

Dash pepper

2 packages (9 ounces *each*) frozen cut
green beans, cooked and drained
(4 cups)

1 can (2.8 ounces) French fried onions

● In 1 ¹/₂-quart casserole, combine soup, milk, soy sauce and pepper. Stir in beans and *¹/₂ can* of the onions.

● Bake at 350°F. for 25 minutes or until hot and bubbling; stir.

● Top with remaining onions. Bake 5 minutes more.

TIP: You may substitute 1 ¹/₂ pounds fresh green beans, cut into 1-inch pieces, cooked and drained, *or* 2 cans (about 16 ounces *each*) cut green beans, drained, for the frozen cut green beans.

Corn and Bean Amandine: Prepare Classic Green Bean Bake as directed above, *except* substitute 1 can (10 ³/₄ ounces) CAMPBELL'S condensed *Golden Corn Soup* for the Cream of Mushroom Soup. Stir in ¹/₄ cup toasted *slivered or sliced almonds* after baking 25 minutes. Top with remaining onions. Continue baking as directed.

Broccoli Bake: Prepare Classic Green Bean Bake as directed above, *except* substitute 1 can (10 ³/₄ ounces) CAMPBELL'S condensed *Cream of Broccoli Soup* for the Cream of Mushroom Soup and 1 package (20 ounces) *frozen broccoli cuts,* cooked and drained, for the green beans.

Makes about 4 ¹/₂ cups or 6 servings.
Prep Time: 10 minutes
Cook Time: 30 minutes

TOMATO, CORN AND BROCCOLI

1 bunch (about 1 ½ pounds) fresh
broccoli, cut up (about 5 cups), *or*
1 package (20 ounces) frozen broccoli
cuts

1 cup water

1 can (10 ¾ ounces) CAMPBELL'S
condensed Golden Corn Soup

½ cup shredded Cheddar cheese
(2 ounces)

¼ cup milk

1 tablespoon snipped fresh basil *or*
1 teaspoon dried basil leaves, crushed

Generous dash pepper

1 cup quartered cherry tomatoes

● In 3-quart saucepan, combine broccoli and
water. Over high heat, heat to boiling. Reduce
heat to low. Cover; cook 8 minutes or until
broccoli is tender-crisp, stirring often. Drain
in colander.

● In same saucepan, combine soup, cheese,
milk, basil and pepper. Return broccoli to
saucepan. Over medium heat, heat through,
stirring occasionally. Stir in tomatoes.

Makes about 5 cups or 8 servings.
Prep Time: 10 minutes
Cook Time: 15 minutes

TOMATO-BASIL ZUCCHINI

1 can (10 ³/₄ ounces) CAMPBELL'S condensed Tomato Soup

¹/₄ cup grated Parmesan cheese

1 tablespoon lemon juice

¹/₂ teaspoon garlic powder

¹/₂ teaspoon dried basil leaves, crushed

6 cups sliced zucchini (about 4 medium)

1 medium green pepper, cut into strips (about 1 cup)

1 large onion, thinly sliced and separated into rings (about 1 cup)

Fresh basil sprig for garnish

● In 5-quart Dutch oven, combine soup, cheese, lemon juice, garlic powder and basil. Over medium heat, heat to boiling, stirring occasionally.

● Add zucchini, green pepper and onion; toss to coat. Cover; cook 15 minutes or until vegetables are tender, stirring often. Garnish with basil, if desired.

Makes about 6 cups or 8 servings.
Prep Time: 10 minutes
Cook Time: 20 minutes

CORN VEGETABLE MEDLEY

1 can (10 ³/₄ ounces) CAMPBELL'S condensed Golden Corn Soup

¹/₂ cup milk

2 cups fresh broccoli flowerets

2 medium carrots, sliced (about 1 cup)

1 cup cauliflowerets

¹/₂ cup shredded Cheddar cheese (2 ounces), optional

● In 2-quart saucepan over medium heat, heat soup and milk to boiling, stirring often. Stir in broccoli, carrots and cauliflowerets.

● Return to boiling. Reduce heat to low. Cover; cook 20 minutes or until vegetables are tender, stirring occasionally. Stir in cheese. Heat through until cheese is melted.

Peppery Vegetable Medley: Prepare Corn Vegetable Medley as directed above, *except* cook ¹/₃ cup diced *sweet red pepper* with the broccoli. Add 1 tablespoon snipped *fresh cilantro* and ¹/₂ to 1 teaspoon *Louisiana-style hot sauce* along with the cheese.

Makes about 3 ¹/₂ cups or 6 servings.
Prep Time: 10 minutes
Cook Time: 25 minutes

CHEDDARY SCALLOPED POTATOES

2 tablespoons margarine *or* butter

1 small onion, sliced and separated into rings (about $1/4$ cup)

1 can (10 $3/4$ ounces) CAMPBELL'S condensed Broccoli Cheese Soup

$1/3$ cup milk

$1/8$ teaspoon pepper

4 medium potatoes (about 1 $1/4$ pounds), cooked and sliced (about 3 $1/2$ cups)

3 slices bacon, cooked and crumbled (optional)

Snipped fresh parsley (optional)

Fresh parsley sprig for garnish

● In 10-inch skillet over medium heat, in hot margarine, cook onion until tender, stirring often.

● Stir in soup, milk and pepper. Add potatoes; stir gently to coat. Heat to boiling. Reduce heat to low. Cover; cook 5 minutes or until hot and bubbling, stirring occasionally. Sprinkle with bacon and snipped parsley. Garnish with parsley sprig, if desired.

TIP: You may substitute 2 cans (about 16 ounces *each*) whole white potatoes, rinsed, drained and sliced, for the fresh potatoes.

Makes about 3 $1/2$ cups or 4 servings.
Prep Time: 25 minutes
Cook Time: 10 minutes

QUICK GAZPACHO

1 can (10 ³/4 ounces) CAMPBELL'S condensed Tomato Soup

1 soup can water

1 tablespoon wine vinegar

1 teaspoon olive oil

¹/4 teaspoon dried basil leaves, crushed

¹/8 teaspoon garlic powder *or* 1 clove garlic, minced

1 medium cucumber, seeded and chopped (about 1 cup)

1 small sweet red *or* green pepper, chopped (about ¹/2 cup)

1 tablespoon chopped onion

● In medium bowl, combine soup, water, vinegar, oil, basil and garlic. Stir in cucumber, red pepper and onion. Cover; refrigerate at least 6 hours or overnight before serving.

Makes about 3 ¹/2 cups or 4 servings.
Prep Time: 15 minutes
Chill Time: 6 hours

TOMATO-VEGETABLE NOODLE SOUP

1 can (10 ³/4 ounces) CAMPBELL'S condensed Tomato Soup

1 soup can water

1 cup cooked mixed vegetables

1 cup cooked bow tie noodles (about 1 cup dry)

● In a 1 ¹/2-quart saucepan, combine soup and water. Add vegetables and noodles. Over medium heat, heat through, stirring occasionally.

Makes about 3 ¹/2 cups or 3 servings.
Prep Time: 5 minutes
Cook Time: 5 minutes

TOMATO-FRENCH ONION SOUP

1 can (10 ³/₄ ounces) CAMPBELL'S condensed Tomato Soup

1 can (10 ¹/₂ ounces) CAMPBELL'S condensed French Onion Soup

2 soup cans water

Toasted bread slices, quartered *or* croutons

Grated Parmesan cheese

● In 2-quart saucepan, combine soups. Add water. Over medium heat, heat through, stirring occasionally.

● Serve in bowls topped with bread; sprinkle with cheese.

Makes about 4 ¹/₂ cups or 5 servings.
Prep Time: 5 minutes
Cook Time: 10 minutes

VEGETABLE CHILI

1 tablespoon olive *or* vegetable oil

1 large onion, chopped (about 1 cup)

1 tablespoon chili powder

¹/₄ teaspoon garlic powder *or* 1 clove garlic, minced

1 package (10 ounces) frozen lima beans *or* whole kernel corn

6 small carrots, diced (about 1 ¹/₂ cups)

¹/₂ cup water

1 can (about 16 ounces) black beans *or* 1 can (about 15 ounces) pinto beans, undrained

1 ¹/₂ cups CAMPBELL'S Tomato Juice

1 can (10 ³/₄ ounces) CAMPBELL'S condensed Golden Mushroom Soup

6 cups hot cooked white rice *or* a combination of white and wild rice

Sour cream (optional)

Sliced green onions (optional)

● In 4-quart Dutch oven or saucepan over medium heat, in hot oil, cook onion, chili powder and garlic powder until onion is tender, stirring often.

● Stir in lima beans, carrots and water. Heat to boiling. Cover; cook 10 minutes or until vegetables are tender, stirring occasionally.

● Stir in black beans, tomato juice and soup. Heat to boiling. Reduce heat to low. Cover; cook 20 minutes, stirring occasionally.

● Serve in bowls over rice. Top with sour cream and sprinkle with green onions.

Makes about 5 ¹/₂ cups or 6 servings.
Prep Time: 10 minutes
Cook Time: 35 minutes

VEGETABLE CHILI

1 In 4-quart Dutch oven over medium heat, in hot oil, cook onion, chili powder and garlic until onion is tender, stirring often.

2 Stir in black beans, tomato juice and soup.

POTATO-CORN CHOWDER

1 tablespoon margarine *or* butter

1 rib celery, chopped (about $^1/_2$ cup)

1 medium onion, chopped (about $^1/_2$ cup)

2 medium potatoes (about $^1/_2$ pound), peeled and diced (about 1 $^1/_2$ cups)

1 cup water

$^1/_8$ teaspoon pepper

1 bay leaf

1 can (10 $^3/_4$ ounces) CAMPBELL'S condensed Golden Corn Soup

1 cup milk

4 slices bacon, cooked and crumbled (optional)

Fresh parsley sprigs for garnish

● In 3-quart saucepan over medium heat, in hot margarine, cook celery and onion until tender, stirring occasionally.

● Add potatoes, water, pepper and bay leaf. Heat to boiling. Reduce heat to low. Cover; cook 15 minutes or until potatoes are tender, stirring occasionally.

● Stir in soup and milk. Cook, uncovered, 5 minutes, stirring occasionally. Discard bay leaf. Serve in bowls. Sprinkle with bacon. Garnish with parsley, if desired.

Seafood-Corn Chowder: Prepare Potato-Corn Chowder as directed above, *except* reduce milk to $^1/_2$ cup. Add 1 cup cut-up *cooked fish or seafood* (clams, oysters, shrimp, salmon or cod) and $^1/_2$ cup *half-and-half* along with the soup.

Makes about 4 $^1/_2$ cups or 4 servings.
Prep Time: 15 minutes
Cook Time: 30 minutes

TACO SOUP

1 can (10 ³/₄ ounces) CAMPBELL'S
  condensed Tomato Soup

1 soup can water

¹/₄ cup salsa

Tortilla chips

Shredded Monterey Jack *or* Cheddar
  cheese

Sliced green onion

Sour cream

● In a 1¹/₂-quart saucepan, combine soup, water and salsa. Over medium heat, heat through, stirring occasionally.

● Serve in bowls with tortilla chips. Sprinkle with cheese and onion. Top with a spoonful of sour cream.

TIP: Salsa is a term for any of a variety of highly seasoned sauces. Uncooked or cooked, these sauces are especially popular in Mexican and Tex-Mex cooking. Salsas are generally chunky in texture and most often contain chili peppers.

Makes about 2 ¹/₂ cups or 2 servings.
Prep Time: 5 minutes
Cook Time: 5 minutes

QUICK LEMON-BROCCOLI RICE

1 can (10 ¹/₂ ounces) CAMPBELL'S condensed Chicken Broth

1 cup small fresh broccoli flowerets

1 small carrot, shredded (about ¹/₃ cup)

1 ¹/₄ cups uncooked quick-cooking rice

2 teaspoons lemon juice

Generous dash pepper

Lemon slices *and* fresh tarragon sprig for garnish

● In 2-quart saucepan over high heat, heat broth to boiling. Add broccoli and carrot. Return to boiling. Reduce heat to low. Cover; cook 5 minutes or until vegetables are tender.

● Stir in rice, lemon juice and pepper. Remove from heat. Cover; let stand 5 minutes or until liquid is absorbed. Fluff rice with fork before serving.

● Garnish with lemon and tarragon, if desired.

Brown Rice with Broccoli: Prepare Quick Lemon-Broccoli Rice as directed above, *except* substitute 1 cup *quick-cooking brown rice*, uncooked, for the quick-cooking rice. Cook rice along with vegetables. Stir in 2 teaspoons snipped *fresh basil leaves or parsley* just before serving.

Makes about 3 cups or 4 servings.
Prep Time: 10 minutes
Cook Time: 15 minutes

VEGETABLE-SEASONED RICE

1 can (14 ¹/₂ ounces) SWANSON Ready To Serve Clear Vegetable Broth

3/4 cup uncooked regular long-grain rice

● In 2-quart saucepan over medium-high heat, heat broth to boiling. Stir in rice.

● Reduce heat to low. Cover; cook 20 minutes or until rice is tender and liquid is absorbed.

Makes about 2 cups or 3 servings.
Prep Time: 5 minutes
Cook Time: 25 minutes

QUICK LEMON-BROCCOLI RICE

*F*IESTA RICE

1 tablespoon vegetable oil

1 small green pepper, chopped
(about ¹/₂ cup)

1 small onion, chopped (about ¹/₄ cup)

3 cups V8 PICANTE *or* LIGHT 'N TANGY
V8 Vegetable Juice

¹/₄ teaspoon garlic powder

1 cup uncooked regular long-grain rice

¹/₂ cup shredded Monterey Jack cheese
(2 ounces)

● In 2-quart saucepan over medium heat, in hot oil, cook pepper and onion until tender, stirring often.

● Add "V8" juice and garlic powder. Heat to boiling. Stir in rice. Reduce heat to low. Cover; cook 15 minutes. Uncover; cook 5 minutes more or until rice is tender and liquid is absorbed, stirring occasionally. Stir in cheese.

Makes about 4 cups or 4 servings.
Prep Time: 10 minutes
Cook Time: 30 minutes

*R*ED RICE AND BEANS

1 tablespoon vegetable oil

1 large onion, chopped (about 1 cup)

¹/₂ teaspoon garlic powder *or* 4 cloves
garlic, minced

¹/₈ teaspoon ground red pepper
(cayenne)

1 cup CAMPBELL'S Tomato Juice

1 can (about 15 ounces) kidney beans,
rinsed and drained

3 cups hot cooked rice

Fresh thyme sprigs for garnish

● In 2-quart saucepan over medium heat, in hot oil, cook onion, garlic and red pepper until onion is tender, stirring occasionally.

● Stir in tomato juice and beans. Heat to boiling. Reduce heat to low. Cover; cook 5 minutes, stirring occasionally. Stir in rice. Heat through. Garnish with thyme, if desired.

TIP: To save time later, cook up some extra rice and save it for another meal. Store the cooked rice in an airtight container in the refrigerator up to 1 week or in the freezer up to 6 months.

Makes about 4 cups or 4 servings.
Prep Time: 20 minutes
Cook Time: 10 minutes

RED RICE AND BEANS

1 Cooked white rice should be tender and moist. Test rice doneness by squeezing a grain between two fingers. Rice is cooked if you can't feel a hard core.

2 Add tomato juice and beans.

3 Add cooked rice. Heat through, stirring occasionally.

SHORTCUT RISOTTO

1 tablespoon margarine *or* butter

1 cup uncooked regular long-grain rice

1 medium onion, chopped
(about $^1/_2$ cup)

1 can (10 $^1/_2$ ounces) CAMPBELL'S
condensed Chicken Broth

1 soup can water

3 tablespoons grated Parmesan cheese

Fresh parsley sprig *and* cherry tomato
slices for garnish

● In 2-quart saucepan over medium-high heat, in hot margarine, cook rice and onion 5 minutes or until rice is browned and onion is tender, stirring constantly.

● Slowly stir in broth and water. Heat to boiling. Reduce heat to low. Cover; cook 20 minutes or until rice is tender and liquid is absorbed.

● Remove from heat. Stir in cheese. Garnish with parsley and tomato, if desired. Makes about 3 cups.

Risotto with Peas: Prepare Shortcut Risotto as directed above, *except* cook $^1/_4$ cup finely chopped *prosciutto* with the rice and onion. Stir in 1 cup *frozen peas* during last 5 minutes of cooking. Garnish with very thin strips *lemon peel*, if desired. Makes about 4 cups.

Risotto Verde: Prepare Shortcut Risotto as directed above, *except* substitute 4 medium *green onions*, sliced (about $^1/_2$ cup), for the chopped onion. Cook 1/4 cup chopped *celery* with the rice and green onions. Stir in 2 cups chopped *fresh spinach* after adding the broth. Garnish with *sweet red pepper strips*, if desired. Make about 4 cups.

Makes 6 servings.
Prep Time: 5 minutes
Cook Time: 30 minutes

QUICK ONION RICE

1 pouch CAMPBELL'S Dry Onion Soup
Mix with Chicken Broth

2 $^1/_2$ cups water

1 cup uncooked regular long-grain rice

● In 2-quart saucepan, combine soup mix and water. Over medium-high heat, heat to boiling.

● Stir in rice. Reduce heat to low. Cover; cook 20 minutes or until rice is tender and liquid is absorbed.

Makes about 3 cups or 3 servings.
Prep Time: 5 minutes
Cook Time: 25 minutes

SHORTCUT RISOTTO (AND VARIATIONS)

CREAMY CHICKEN-BROCCOLI RICE

1 can (10 ³/₄ ounces) CAMPBELL'S condensed Cream of Chicken & Broccoli Soup

1 ¹/₂ cups water

¹/₈ teaspoon pepper

³/₄ cup uncooked regular long-grain rice

Fresh sage leaves *and* tomato slices for garnish

● In 2-quart saucepan, combine soup, water and pepper. Over medium-high heat, heat to boiling.

● Stir in rice. Reduce heat to low. Cover; cook 25 minutes or until rice is tender and mixture is creamy, stirring often. Garnish with fresh sage and tomato, if desired.

Makes about 3 cups or 6 servings.
Prep Time: 5 minutes
Cook Time: 30 minutes

VEGETABLE-RICE PILAF

1 tablespoon margarine *or* butter

¾ cup uncooked regular long-grain rice

¼ teaspoon dried basil leaves, crushed

1 can (14 ½ ounces) SWANSON Ready To Serve Clear Vegetable Broth

¾ cup frozen peas and carrots

¼ cup chopped sweet red pepper

Fresh basil sprig for garnish

● In 2-quart saucepan over medium-high heat, in hot margarine, cook rice and dried basil until rice is browned, stirring constantly.

● Stir in broth. Heat to boiling. Reduce heat to low. Cover; cook 10 minutes. Stir in peas and carrots and pepper. Cover; cook 10 minutes or until rice is tender and liquid is absorbed. Garnish with fresh basil, if desired.

Makes about 3 ½ cups or 4 servings.
Prep Time: 5 minutes
Cook Time: 25 minutes

ALL-TIME FAVORITE BARBECUE SAUCE

1 can (10 ³/₄ ounces) CAMPBELL'S
  condensed Tomato Soup

¹/₄ cup vinegar

¹/₄ cup vegetable oil

2 tablespoons packed brown sugar

1 tablespoon Worcestershire sauce

1 teaspoon garlic powder

¹/₈ teaspoon Louisiana-style hot sauce
  (optional)

● In small bowl, combine soup, vinegar, oil, brown sugar, Worcestershire sauce, garlic powder and hot sauce; set aside.

● Use sauce to baste ribs, chicken, hamburgers or steak during broiling or grilling.

Serving Suggestion: All-Time Favorite Barbecue Sauce is brushed on a broiled chicken leg and accompanied with cooked corn on the cob and mixed salad greens. Garnish with fresh basil.

Makes about 1 ¹/₃ cups sauce.
Prep Time: 5 minutes

CREAMY MUSHROOM SAUCE

1 can (10 ³/₄ ounces) CAMPBELL'S
  condensed Cream of Mushroom Soup

¹/₃ cup milk *or* water

● In 1-quart saucepan, combine soup and milk. Over medium heat, heat through, stirring often. Serve over hot cooked vegetables or roast beef.

TIP: To microwave sauce, in 1-quart microwave-safe casserole, combine soup and milk. Microwave, uncovered, on HIGH 2 ¹/₂ minutes or until hot and bubbling, stirring halfway through heating.

Makes about 1 ¹/₂ cups sauce.
Prep Time: 5 minutes
Cook Time: 5 minutes

ALL-TIME FAVORITE BARBECUE SAUCE

EASY CRANBERRY SAUCE

1 container (14 ounces) MARIE'S Glaze
   for Strawberries

1 package (12 ounces) fresh *or* frozen
   cranberries (about 3 cups)

$1/2$ cup orange juice

1 tablespoon sugar (optional)

● In 2-quart saucepan, combine glaze, berries and juice. Over medium-high heat, heat to boiling. Reduce heat to low. Cook 10 minutes or until berries are soft, stirring often.

● Remove from heat. Pour into bowl. Cover; refrigerate at least 2 hours before serving. (For sweeter sauce, stir in sugar.) Serve with cooked pork, ham or poultry. Refrigerate any remaining sauce.

Serving Suggestion: Easy Cranberry Sauce is spooned over a broiled pork chop. Garnish with orange slices and fresh thyme sprig. Serve with hot cooked orzo and green beans.

Makes about 3 cups sauce.
Prep Time: 5 minutes
Cook Time: 15 minutes
Chill Time: 2 hours

CHEDDAR CHEESE SAUCE

1 can (10 ³/₄ ounces) CAMPBELL'S condensed Cheddar Cheese Soup

¹/₃ cup milk

● In 1-quart saucepan, combine soup and milk. Over low heat, heat through, stirring often. Serve over hot cooked vegetables, French fries or omelets.

Cheese Sauce Dijonnaise: Prepare Cheddar Cheese Sauce as directed above, *except* add 1 tablespoon *Dijon-style mustard* to the soup mixture.

Serving Suggestion: Cheddar Cheese Sauce is spooned over steak fries then sprinkled with paprika. Garnish with fresh parsley.

Makes about 1 ¹/₂ cups sauce.
Prep Time: 5 minutes
Cook Time: 5 minutes

PINEAPPLE-PEACH DIPPING SAUCE

1 can (about 8 ounces) crushed pineapple in juice, undrained

¹/₂ cup MARIE'S Glaze for Peaches

¹/₂ teaspoon grated fresh ginger *or* ¹/₄ teaspoon ground ginger

● In small bowl, combine *undrained* pineapple, glaze and ginger. Cover; refrigerate until serving time. Use sauce as a dip for hot egg rolls or chicken nuggets or use to baste chicken or ribs during broiling or grilling.

TIP: Fresh ginger can be found in the produce section of most supermarkets and in Oriental markets. When buying fresh ginger (gingerroot), select a piece that's firm and heavy; avoid shriveled pieces. To store, wrap and refrigerate up to 1 week or freeze up to 3 months. Purchase ground ginger as you do other spices and store in cool, dry dark place.

Makes about 1 ¹/₂ cups sauce.
Prep Time: 5 minutes

ORANGE-MUSTARD SAUCE

1 cup V8 Vegetable Juice

¹/₂ cup orange marmalade

1 tablespoon Dijon-style mustard

● In 1¹/₂-quart saucepan, combine "V8" juice, marmalade and mustard. Over medium-high heat, heat to boiling. Reduce heat to low; cook 10 minutes or until sauce thickens, stirring often.

● Use sauce to baste chicken, pork chops or turkey cutlets during the last few minutes of broiling or grilling.

Makes about 1 cup sauce.
Prep Time: 5 minutes
Cook Time: 15 minutes

PINEAPPLE-PEACH DIPPING SAUCE

GINGER-CRANBERRY SAUCE

1 can (8 ounces) jellied cranberry
   sauce, cut into cubes

3/4 cup refrigerated MARIE'S Tangy
   French Dressing and Dip

1 tablespoon soy sauce

1 teaspoon ground ginger

1 teaspoon garlic powder

1/8 teaspoon ground red pepper
   (cayenne)

● In 1-quart saucepan, combine cranberry sauce, dressing, soy sauce, ginger, garlic and red pepper. Over medium heat, heat until cranberry sauce is melted, stirring often.

● Remove from heat. Pour into bowl. Cool to room temperature. Use sauce to glaze ham during last 30 minutes of heating or serve as a sauce for cooked ham, pork or poultry. Refrigerate any remaining sauce.

Serving Suggestion: Ginger-Cranberry Sauce is used to glaze ham-and-vegetable kabobs.

Makes about 1 1/2 cups sauce.
Prep Time: 5 minutes
Cook Time: 10 minutes
Cool Time: 30 minutes

CHICKEN-BROCCOLI SAUCE

1 can (10 3/4 ounces) CAMPBELL'S
   condensed Cream of
   Chicken & Broccoli Soup

1/2 cup milk

1/8 teaspoon pepper

● In 1-quart saucepan, combine soup, milk and pepper. Over medium heat, heat through, stirring often. Serve over broiled or grilled chicken or hot cooked rice or noodles.

Makes about 1 1/2 cups sauce.
Prep Time: 5 minutes
Cook Time: 5 minutes

GINGER-CRANBERRY SAUCE

EASY VEGETABLE SAUCE

1/4 cup margarine *or* butter

1/4 cup all-purpose flour

1 can (14 1/2 ounces) SWANSON Ready
  To Serve Clear Vegetable Broth

1/2 cup milk

Salt

Pepper

● In 2-quart saucepan over medium heat, melt margarine. Stir in flour until smooth.

● Gradually stir in broth and milk. Cook until mixture boils and thickens, stirring constantly. Season to taste with salt and pepper. Serve over hot cooked vegetables.

Makes about 2 cups sauce.
Prep Time: 5 minutes
Cook Time: 5 minutes

ANYTIME BROCCOLI-CHEESE SAUCE

1 can (10 3/4 ounces) CAMPBELL'S
  condensed Broccoli Cheese Soup

1/3 cup milk

● In 1-quart saucepan, combine soup and milk. Over medium heat, heat through, stirring often. Serve over cooked meat, poultry, fish, vegetables, rice or noodles.

Parmesan Broccoli Sauce: Prepare Broccoli Cheese Sauce as directed above, *except* add 1/4 cup grated *Parmesan cheese* with the soup.

Creamy Broccoli Sauce: Prepare Broccoli Cheese Sauce as directed above, *except* in 1-quart saucepan gradually stir soup into *half* of a 3-ounce package *cream cheese*, softened; stir in milk.

TIP: To soften cream cheese, remove foil wrapping and place on microwave-safe plate. Microwave, uncovered, on HIGH 20 seconds or until soft.

Makes about 1 1/2 cups sauce.
Prep Time: 5 minutes
Cook Time: 5 minutes

RECIPE INDEX

RECIPES BY PRODUCT INDEX

Campbell's Tomato Juice
Barbecue Burgers, 35
Carrot-Spice Muffins, 45
Cinnamon Carrots, 158
Greek-Style Beef 'n' Mac Bake, 126
Italian Chicken and Pasta, 116
Italian Vegetables and Pasta, 134
Red Rice and Beans, 172
Shrimp Creole, 114
Sweet 'n' Saucy Chops, 108
Two-Bean Chili, 92
Vegetable Chili, 166

Franco-American Gravy
Beefed-Up Chili, 92
Burgundy Beef, 87
Herbed Turkey and Mushrooms, 78
Homestyle Chicken and Biscuits, 73
Hot Turkey Sandwiches, 32
Lemon Chicken Primavera, 62
Orange-Glazed Turkey, 80
Quick and Easy Stir-Fry, 95
Quick Beef Stroganoff, 91
Santa Fe Chili Chicken, 48
Sausage and Peppers, 100
Skillet Rosemary Potatoes, 152
Turkey and Stuffing Bake, 83

Marie's Dressing and Dip
Bacon Bagel Snacks, 18
Bistro Chicken Salad, 138
Buffalo Wings, 18
Caesar Bean Salad, 150
California Pizza Breads, 42
Chicken and Pasta Salad, 143
Chicken El Paso, 48
Garden Chicken Salad, 146
Ginger-Cranberry Sauce, 184
Parmesan Bread Deluxe, 44
Poppy Seed Fruit Dip, 26
White Pizza Muffins, 40

Marie's Fruit Glaze
Apples 'n' Cinnamon Topping, 28
Banana Split Cake, 30
Blueberry-Crunch Parfaits, 24
Blueberry-Peach Sundaes, 29
Chocolate-Banana Cream Pie, 24
Coconut-Marshmallow Fruit Salad, 151
Easy Cranberry Sauce, 180
Glazed Fruit Salad, 151
Glazed Sweet Potatoes, 160
Pineapple-Peach Dipping Sauce, 182
Strawberry Angel Dessert, 30

Marie's Zesty Fat Free Vinaigrette
Chicken Fajitas, 98
Lentil-Rice Salad, 149
Oriental Beef Salad, 140
Pork Fajitas, 98
Tangy Broiled Chicken, 50
Tortellini Salad, 142

Pepperidge Farm (Cookies, Crackers, Croutons
  and Stuffings)
Banana Split Cake, 30
Bistro Chicken Salad, 138
Broccoli-Cheese Dip, 15
Fruited Pork Stuffing Bake, 102
Garden Turkey and Stuffing, 83
Mexican Chicken Dip, 14
Pork and Corn Stuffing Bake, 102
Turkey and Stuffing Bake, 83

Prego Pizza Sauce
Chicken Pizza Muffins, 39
Deep-Dish Pizza, 40
Garden Pita Pizzas, 42
Pizza Fondue, 12

Prego Spaghetti Sauce
Chicken Parmesan, 47
Extra-Easy Lasagna, 122
Mussels Marinara, 16
Pork Chops Italiano, 100
Ravioli and Sausage, 128
Spaghetti Pie, 134

**Swanson Premium Chunk White Chicken
  or Turkey**
Barbecued Chicken Sandwiches, 38
Chicken and Pasta Salad, 143
Chicken and Vegetable Stir-Fry, 76
Chicken-Broccoli Divan, 70
Chicken Pizza Muffins, 39
Chicken Quesadillas, 36
Chicken Salad Sandwiches, 38
Chinese Chicken Salad, 144
Country Chicken Soup, 77
Curried Chicken Spread, 14
Easy Chicken Enchiladas, 74
Garden Chicken Salad, 146
Garden Turkey and Stuffing, 83
Homestyle Chicken and Biscuits, 73
Mexican Chicken Dip, 14
Turkey and Stuffing Bake, 83
Turkey Tetrazzini, 120

Swanson Ready to Serve Clear Broth
Chicken and Vegetable Stir-Fry, 76
Chicken-Mushroom Risotto, 68
Country Chicken Soup, 77
Easy Vegetable Sauce, 186
Glazed Vegetables, 156
Orange-Glazed Chicken, 52
Oriental Chicken and Noodles, 64
Vegetable-Rice Pilaf, 177
Vegetable-Seasoned Rice, 170

V8 Vegetable Juice
Bloody Eight, 22
Cranberry Sipper, 23
Fiesta Rice, 172
Frosty Gazpacho, 23
Fruit Warmer, 20
Light 'n Tangy Twister, 21
Orange Mist, 20
Orange-Mustard Sauce, 182
Spicy Hot Refresher, 20
Sunshine Punch, 22
Tangy Broiled Chicken, 50
Tangy Mulled Cider, 23
Tropical Slush, 22

Vlasic or Early California Olives
California Pizza Breads, 42
Garden Chicken Salad, 146
Nachos, 12
Spanish Chicken and Mushrooms, 57